AMERICAN
MOTORSPORTS

THIS IS A CARLTON BOOK

Copyright © Carlton Books Limited 1997

This edition published in 1997 by
Chartwell Books, and imprint of
Book Sales Inc.
114 Northfield Avenue, Edison, N.J.

10 9 8 7 6 5 4 3 2 1

Produced by Carlton Books Limited,
20 St Anne's Court
Wardour Street, London W1V 3AW

Catalog-in-Publication Data for this book is available upon request

ISBN 0 7858 0716 0

Project Editor: Simon Kirrane
Production: Garry Lewis, Neil Williams

Printed in Dubai

AMERICAN
MOTORSPORTS

CHARTWELL
BOOKS, INC.

CONTENTS

Drag Racing 102

Off-Road Motor Sports 134

Sports Car Racing 154

Dirt Track 170

Statistics 184

Acknowledgments and Index 190

INTRODUCTION

America boasts the richest tapestry of motor sports endeavor on the planet. While other countries can rightly claim noteworthy legacies in one form of auto racing or another, no other land can match the United States for the sheer diversity, scope and size of its motor sports scene. On Memorial Day weekend, for example, as many as half a million souls jam the Indianapolis Motor Speedway to witness the Indianapolis 500—the world's largest single day sporting event crowd. Some 700 miles southeast of Indianapolis lies the Charlotte Motor Speedway, where another a few hundred thousand celebrate 'Decoration Day' at the year's longest stock car race, NASCAR's Coca-Cola 600.

The competition runs over to Monday in the hamlet of Lime Rock, Connecticut, where local zoning laws prohibit racing on Sundays. Thus the sports car crowd enjoys a long weekend as some of the world's most exotic sports prototypes tackle the hills and dales of the picturesque New England road course.

And that's just one holiday weekend. On a normal summer weekend—indeed on many a weekday—hundreds of races take place across the United States on the dirt ovals, permanent road courses, bull rings, high banked speedways and drag strips that dot the American landscape. In the case of the SCORE and HDRA series, the competition even spills 'off road' in events pitting phenomenally durable machines against one another over some of the harshest terrain and in some of the most brutal conditions known to Mankind.

Ironically, the very diversity that makes motor sports appealing to such a cross section of America has conspired to keep racing from challenging the traditional stick and ball sports for a place in the hearts and minds of the mass media. Although auto racing as a whole ranks at (or near) the top of attendance in American sports, the segmentation of the fan base into drag racing fans, Indy car fans, sports car fans, dirt car fans, off-road racing fans and stock car fans—none of which individually match the likes of baseball, football or basketball in attendance and television ratings—long consigned auto racing to the ranks of America's under-reported sports.

In recent years, however, the marketing programs associated with the commercial sponsorship necessary to offset the astronomical cost of racing have helped boost the sport's profile. Also, the emergence of increasingly specialized media like cable television networks, as well as new nationwide general interest publications such as *USA Today*, has enabled motor sports—led by NASCAR's Winston Cup series—to gain a foothold in the national sports awareness.

Lurking just over the horizon are technological and sociological forces that may well provide motor sports with the energy to assume a leading role in the sporting consciousness of future generations. The emerging field of video and virtual reality games appears uniquely suited to auto racing's blend of physical talents, mental skills and technical know-how, for example. And in an age when sportsmanship, integrity and grace are increasingly rare attributes in the traditional sports, most racing participants are model citizens. To be sure, their behavior is in no small part a result of their keenly-honed sensitivity to the needs of their sponsors. But at a time when the terms "athlete" and "role model" are all but mutually exclusive, the public image of its leading figures gives auto racing another exciting opportunity to win over new fans of all ages.

Predictions of auto racing's ascendancy on the American sports scene are nothing new, of course. Auto racing was to be 'Sport of the '70s' before the Oil Crisis and a host of other forces conspired to stunt its growth. But with a new generation of motor sports facilities sprouting up from Disney World to Fontana, from California to New Hampshire, from Las Vegas to Colorado Springs; with more than 15 million people attending races in 1996 and with a new generation of fans coming of age at a time when racing is no longer relegated to the agate section of the newspapers, the future of American auto racing has never looked better.

David Phillips
General Editor

THE BRICKYARD 400 *Thanks to institutions like this one throughout every motor sport, America is a richly diverse melting pot of motoring endeavor.*

THE ORIGINS OF AMERICAN MOTOR SPORT

Early American Racing and the Birth of the National Championship

As with the nation itself, America's motor sports originate from Europe, where the first organized competition for 'carriages without horses' took the form of an 80-mile reliability run over primitive public roads between Paris and Rouen on July 22, 1894. Intriguingly, motor sports' first controversy erupted when the second automobile across the finish line—a Daimler-powered Peugeot driven by Claude LeMaitre—was judged the winner, since it was more in keeping with the spirit of the automobile than the first finisher, a steam-powered machine driven by the Count de Dion.

A more ambitious trial was held the following summer between Paris and Bordeaux, but it was not until late Fall of 1895 that America's first auto race took place. Originally scheduled for November 2, the race from Chicago to Waukegan and back was postponed until Thanksgiving Day, owing to the entrants' general state of unreadiness. Thus was another long-standing racing tradition born.

The race took place in horrendous conditions, as a foot of snow had blanketed the Chicago area prior to the event. The winning Duryea, driven by Oscar Mueller with relief from Charles King, averaged a blis-tering 6.66 mph over the 54-mile run. The following year, a point-to-point race sponsored by Cosmopolitan magazine was held between New York City and Irvingtown-on-Hudson, and in 1896 American auto racing made its debut on a closed circuit, in this case the horse race track in Naragansett Park at the Rhode Island State Fair.

Before long, races were staged at converted dirt tracks in Chicago, Cleveland, Minneapolis, Indianapolis, St Louis, Detroit, Philadelphia, and New York City, while hillclimbs were also gaining in popularity, most notably the Mount Washington Hillclimb which dates back to 1904. This early era of racing produced America's first legitimate racing hero in Barney Oldfield. The former bicycle champion turned to automobiles in 1902 and soon won races throughout the midwest and the east coast, becoming the first driver to lap a mile-long oval track in under a minute.

America's early contributions to racing were not restricted to the competition itself. Newspaper publisher Gordon Bennett sponsored a series of competitions in France from 1900–1905 that proved to be the forerunners of the first French Grand Prix in 1906. Back home, the early Automobile Club of America was being superseded by the Automobile Association of America (AAA).

A QUIET DRIVE IN THE COUNTRY *A racer, with a serene air, at Watkins Glen in 1949.*

MAINTAINING INTEGRITY *Wooden board tracks were better than tarmac in the early days as the latter tended to disintegrate.*

It was under the AAA's auspices that William K. Vanderbilt, great grandson of Commodore Vanderbilt and an accomplished driver himself, having twice set landspeed records, began the great tradition of the Vanderbilt Cup races in 1904 with a ten-lap race around a 30-mile road course on Long Island, featuring an international field of drivers and automobiles. An estimated 50,000 spectators saw American expatriate George Heath win the first event in a French Panhard, at an average speed of 52.2 mph.

Such was the success of the event that upwards of 200,000 people flocked to the following year's Vanderbilt Cup, with subsequent races attracting throngs of such magnitude that crowd control became a serious problem. After two mechanics were killed and dozens of spectators injured in the 1910 race, it was moved to Savannah for the next year, and later to Milwaukee, Santa Monica, and San Francisco, before it was discontinued after 1916.

Nor were the Vanderbilt races the only major road races of the early

1900s. As many as 400,000 people attended the Quaker City Motor Club's Founders' Day races in Fairmount Park, Philadelphia, while Elgin, Illinois, hosted a long-running series of road events beginning in 1910. The American Prize races in Savannah that began in 1908 actually outstripped the Vanderbilt Cup races in prestige. Unlike the Vanderbilt events on Long Island, which were held on public roads often in deplorable condition, the American Prize was contested on roadways meticulously maintained

by labor gangs. What's more, the Georgia state militia patrolled the course to keep the estimated 100,000-strong crowds in order.

Racing reached its apogee in Savannah in 1911, when both the Vanderbilt Cup and American Prize races were held. Officials declined to hold either race the following year in the face of growing criticism from the local populace over the inconvenience caused by the closure of public roads, as well as the use of convict labor to maintain the race course.

As many of the great early races

BONESHAKERS *These 1911 Indy cars instill little confidence.*

faded from the scene, others took their place. Santa Monica was the site of some of America's greatest road races from 1911–1916, while the board tracks that would go on to be the focus of post-World War I racing in America were beginning to sprout up around the country. In Indianapolis, meanwhile, a group of local businessmen headed by Carl Fisher were building a 2.5-mile rectangular course envisioned as both a race track and a proving ground for the automotive industry, much of which was located in the Indianapolis area.

After a disastrous debut in 1909, in which the crushed stone and tar track surface broke apart, the Indianapolis Motor Speedway was repaved with bricks. A series of races

was held, varying in length from 50–200 miles in May, 1910, whereupon the owners decided to hold a single 500-mile event on Memorial Day, 1911. The inaugural Indy 500 was won by Ray Harroun in his Marmon Wasp and soon after the AAA inaugurated its official national championship.

Although some modern records show that the first national championship was won by George Robertson in 1909, most historians agree that the AAA did not begin actively promoting a national championship until 1916. In fact, the earlier 'national champions' resulted not from an officially-sanctioned series of races but rather the work of Motor Age magazine's editors, who

SPOILS FOR THE VICTOR *Along with speed and excitement there are other benefits. Here 1958 Indy 500 winner Jimmy Bryan gets a kiss from starlet Shirley Maclaine.*

DANGEROUS GAME *As the flag is flashed for the 1955 Indy 500 no one knew the two-time winner of the previous finals, Bill Vukovich, would perish in a crash.*

compiled early race statistics.

Although the Indianapolis Motor Speedway did not hold its 500-mile races during America's involvement in World War I, the national championship continued on a mixture of dirt, board and concrete ovals; by this stage, race promoters had discovered it was far easier to collect admission fees for an enclosed track than in the open countryside of the road races, while the fans benefited by seeing the entire course.

Although the AAA series would suffer another hiccup of sorts in 1920, where records dispute whether Tommy Milton or Gaston Chevrolet was victorious, the national champi-onship gained momentum through the golden era of the 1920s when the likes of Milton, Jimmy Murphy, Earl Cooper, Louis Meyer and Frank Lockhart raced fleets of Duesenbergs and Millers on the nation's tracks.

The economic woes of the Great Depression saw a shrinking of the national championship's stature but, after a four-year hiatus during World War II, it was rescued in 1946. After the AAA bowed out of the auto rac-ing in 1955, the championship was taken over by the United States Auto Club until 1979, when Championship Auto Racing Teams established the PPG Indy Car World Series which continues to this day.

LEGENDS *Indy racing has thrust greatness upon many throughout its history. Two of the best examples of this are A.J. Foyt, (above) and Michael Andretti (bottom).*

Dirt Track Racing's Legacy

Dirt tracks are part of the fabric of American motor sport, dating back to the races at Naragansett. Indeed, the Milwaukee Mile—which operated as a dirt track from 1903 until it was paved in 1954—predates the Indianapolis Motor Speedway by six years.

The dirt tracks really came to prominence in the 1930s after the demise of maintenance-intensive board tracks. Indeed, but for the Brickyard at Indianapolis, virtually every event on the AAA national championship calendar from 1932 through the mid-'30s was contested on dirt, including the Pike's Peak hillclimb, which was a part of the national championship as late as 1969.

Beginning in the 1950s, however, an increasing number of track owners succumbed to the lure of pavement. First came Milwaukee, then the new track in Trenton, Phoenix, followed in 1965 by Langhorne. At Sacramento, 1970, Al Unser won the last national championship race held on a dirt track.

The disappearance of dirt tracks from the USAC national championship hardly signalled their demise, however. Hundreds, perhaps thousands, of dirt tracks dot the American countryside to this day, hosting local events each summer weekend. Once or twice a year the best tracks attract the headliners of the World of Outlaws and, in the midwest, USAC's flourishing sprint car, midget, and champ dirt car divisions, while the California Racing Association offers a similar agenda for a host of tracks out west.

The top drivers, like Steve Kinser and Sammy Swindell, earn hundreds of thousands of dollars a year from T-shirt sales alone, while traveling from bull ring to bull ring, racing two, three, and more times a week in one of motor sport's most physically—and mentally—demanding arenas.

ROUGH RIDING *This shot of Stock Car racing shows the problems inherent with a combination of speed, cars and basic tracks.*

Speed Records from Daytona to Bonneville

Throughout the early years of American motor sport, speed record attempts on beaches and frozen rivers and lakes proved as popular as road and closed track races. Favored sites for the attempts included many New Jersey beaches, as well as those in Rhode Island and Texas. But the predominant setting for speed records was the stretch between Ormond and Daytona Beach, Florida, where in 1903 Alexander Winton covered a measured mile in 68.9 mph in his Winton Bullet. The following year, William K. Vanderbilt earned a place in the record books when his Mercedes reached 92.3 mph over a mile-long section of Ormond Beach.

Largely at the behest of Vanderbilt, the Ormond-Daytona Beach became the site of an annual international speed trial competition, which attracted entries from across America and Europe. In 1906, Fred Marriott obliterated all existing marks with a run of 127.66 mph in his steam-powered Stanley Rocket. The following year, Marriott was seriously injured when he crashed trying to improve upon his record, and it was not until 1910 that it was bettered by the redoubtable Barney Oldfield, who posted a run of 131.72 mph in his Blitzen-Benz.

Europe became the capital of the speed world until the beaches of England were declared off-limits in the wake of Parry Thomas's fatal accident in Wales in the early 1900s. Sir Malcolm Campbell thus came to Daytona in 1928 with his Bluebird and established a new record of 203.96 mph. His mark stood for just two months before Ray Keech upped the ante to 207.55 mph in his tri-engined White-Triplex.

Daytona Beach continued to be the focus of landspeed record attempts until the mid-1930s when, after a series of fatal accidents—including that of Indy 500 winner Frank Lockhart—attention shifted to Utah's Bonneville Salt Flats. Bonneville has since gone on to become the world's center of speed record activity.

The Beginnings of Drag Racing

The desert would also spawn two distinctly American motor sports in drag racing and off-road racing. Following World War II, the dry lake beds of the Mojave Desert east of Los Angeles became the center of the hot rod phenomenon—at least the legal part of it. Much illegal street racing took place on the boulevards and freeways of Southern California.

In 1951, Wally Parks, editor of Hot Rod Magazine, founded the National Hot Rod Association as a means of organizing drag racing activities into legal, manageable racing. By that point, the first private drag racing strips were opening up around the country, featuring the uniquely American form of racing where two cars pair off and race side-by-side over a quarter-mile stretch of pavement.

The spot quickly developed a myriad of classes based upon performance and appearance. The three most important classes to emerge in the burgeoning professional drag racing scene of the 1970s and '80s were Top Fuel, Funny Cars, and Pro Stock, even as the sport produced icons like Don 'Big Daddy' Garlits, Don Prudhomme, and Tommy Ivo.

Today's nitro-burning top fuelers routinely traverse the quarter-mile in under five seconds with a top speed well in excess of 300 mph, with the Funny Cars not far behind in elapsed time and top speed. The NHRA's premiere Winston Drag Racing series annually attracts nearly two million fans, and just as Memorial Day has long been synonymous with the Indianapolis 500, so Labor Day is associated with the NHRA's National, held each September a few miles down the road from the Indianapolis Motor Speedway in Clermont, Indiana's Indianapolis Raceway Park.

OVER: WE HAVE LIFT-OFF... *Drag racer Eddie Hill thrusts his 1996 Top Fueler forwards... and skywards.*

A REALLY HOT SPORT *The early drag racers had many problems to content with as this early Top Fueler, with exploding engine, illustrates.*

Off-Road Racing Origins

Just as the dry lakes of the Mojave Desert proved the perfect locale for the hot rodders of the 1940s and '50s, so its harsh and demanding terrain would also give birth to off-road racing in the 1960s and '70s. While many motor sports are tied in with the advent of the petrol-engine vehicles and quickly swathed themselves in rules and regulatory bodies there has always been a more loosely governed tradition running in tandem. That is, of races occurring where the ingredients appear to be little more than, available space, available vehicles and speed fever to spare. Off-road racing, although stemming from the traditions of fun racing has, increasingly in recent years, garnered more officialdom, sponsorship, media coverage and fans.

In the late '30s the advent of the Jeep, a name formed by the phonetic linking of the initials GP (for general purpose), unwittingly sowed the seeds for this sport. Following the war the vehicles, that in war time had a life expectancy of just six weeks, were so popular that many ex-servicemen were keen to try them out on rough terrain and under more peaceful conditions.

Also, just as the dry lakes of the Mojave Desert proved the perfect locale for the hot rodders of the 1940s and '50s, so its harsh demanding terrain would encourage off-road racing in the 1960s and '70s. This combined with the refinement of another vehicle, the Volkswagen Beetle (aka 'The Bug'). This light and easily modified car adapted to desert and beach racing well and set the standards for many of the vehicles that were to come to off-road in its wake.

Off-roading in the '90s is still evolving and mutating. Rules and regulatory bodies may well spring up but just as surely as they do another development of the sport emerges. Indeed of the countless racing disciplines that fall under the umbrella term of off-road, there is only one rule that is now strictly followed and vehemently enforced by all and that is conservation. Though it has its critics off-roaders are keen to show themselves to be working with nature and not against it. As a result there is a growth in off-road racing facilities and of course racers to use them.

As the sport continues to spread tendrils in every directions and as media coverage seems ever more ready to report the sport to its growing army of fans it is good to see that the ungoverned spirit that created the sport, while still an essential force, has grown up and knows and accepts responsibility.

The Birth of Stock Car Racing

Meanwhile, back in Florida, as one chapter in Daytona Beach's motor sports history ended with the westward shift of the speed record attempts in the mid-1930s, so another began with the introduction of stock car racing on a makeshift circuit employing the beach and an adjacent stretch of US Highway 1-A. The elongated oval featured parallel mile-and-a-half straightaways on the beach and highway, joined at each end by roads a tenth of a mile long.

The AAA sanctioned the inaugural event in 1936, but the scheduled 250-miler had to be reduced to 200 when the connecting roads deteriorated to the point that they became virtually impassable. The race was won by Milt Marion in a 1-2-3-4-5 sweep for Ford, the fifth placed car piloted by one Bill France, who would go on to have a singular impact on future racing at Daytona Beach and across America.

In addition to racing stock cars, France had established a reputation as a savvy stock car racing promoter throughout the southeast in the 1930s. Following World War II, France founded the National Association of Stock Car Auto Racing (NASCAR) and organized its first championship in 1948, which consisted of a race at Daytona Beach, followed by events at dirt tracks along the eastern seaboard. The NASCAR series soon grew to more than a dozen races and, in 1950, featured its first 500-mile race, on a paved track at Darlington Speedway.

NASCAR continued to grow through the 1950s as more and more modern paved speedways came on line from Daytona to Charlotte, Atlanta, and Rockingham, while old dirt tracks like Martinsville and North Wilkesboro went to pavement. Although the balance of its activity was concentrated in the southeast, NASCAR went on to create a Western Division and then, in 1971, NASCAR established one of auto racing's most lucrative and long-lived sponsorship agreements with the R.J. Reynolds Tobacco Company, an association that spurred the renamed Winston Cup Series to unparalleled levels of success in the 1980s and into the '90s.

Surface tension *Dale Earnhardt and Jeff Gordon battle it out in the NAPA 500.*

CAR 43 WHERE ARE YOU? *Lee Petty takes his car in for a rapid service as the fans look on.*

WEALTHY BENEFACTORS *Motor sports, in any of its various forms would not survive if not for sponsors plastering cars, such as this Porsche, with their adverts.*

The Rebirth of Road Racing

Just as modern stock car racing had its origins in the immediate aftermath of World War II, so road racing—which, apart from a two-year revival of the Vanderbilt Cup races at the colossal Roosevelt Raceway on Long Island, was in virtual hibernation during the 1920s and '30s—began its long comeback in the late-1940s. Although the Automobile Racing Club of America had kept road racing on life support through the '30s, it was the Sports Car Club of America—founded by Ted Robertson in Boston, 1944—which sparked its revival.

Initially, the SCCR had more interest in preserving old sports cars than racing them. But in 1948 the SCCR organized its first major sports car race, held on a daunting 6.6-mile road course in and around Watkins Glen, New York. The race was won by Frank Griswold in an Alfa Romeo and, before long, the SCCR sanctioned road races from Elkhart Lake, Wisconsin, to Bridgehampton, NY, and later, Torrey Pines and Pebble Beach, Costa Rica.

In 1953, the SCCA's 12-hour endurance race on the airport circuit at Sebring, Florida, was recognized as part of the World Sports Car Championship. With the assistance of Air Force General Curtis Le May, SCCR races proliferated on the runways of various Air Force bases during the 1950s, even as permanent road circuits began appearing at places like Riverside, and Lime Rock, while still others replaced the open road courses at Watkins Glen, Elkhart Lake, and Bridgehampton.

The SCCR clung to its amateur roots until the early 1960s, when it began sanctioning professional sports car racing. Its professional racing series then grew in leaps and bounds to include the Canadian-America Challenge Cup for unlimited sports cars, the Formula 5000 championship for 5-liter open wheel cars, and the Trans-Am championship for modified American pony cars, the latter continuing to this day as the SCCA's professional racing flagship series.

The SCCR also produced the offshoot International Motor Sports Association (IMSR), created when John Bishop left to form his own series for sports cars in 1971. The IMSR ultimately became America's leading professional sports car racing organization in the 1980s, when it sanctioned the Daytona 24 Hour race and the 12 Hours of Sebring. These races formed part of the internationally-renowned IMSR Camel GT Championship, precursor to today's Exxon World Sports Car Championship, sanctioned by IMSR's successor, Professional Sports Car Racing.

OVERLEAF: ALL CHANGE *If a driver is going to win in any motor sport he has to battle against his major enemy… time. Many a race has been won and lost in the pit lane and in this rapid 1997 CART tire change, the pressure is on.*

A WING AND A PRAYER *The Chaparral with its innovative air flow wing stands out from the crowd at this Can-Am race at Riverside in 1967.*

STOCK CAR RACING

In the annals of American motor sports, no form of auto racing has enjoyed such popularity and interest as NASCAR's major league Winston Cup.

This form of racing, like many, sprang from humble roots but has grown to its present status through competition between the kind of machines that people in the grandstands and television viewers can identify with. The cars resemble, at least on the surface, the type of car the public drives to work, to school, and to the grocery store. They are driven with such skill and deceptive ease by the larger-than-life daredevils that it looks sufficiently easy for the average fan to feel that, given the opportunity, they too could go on the track and race with the big boys. Despite this impression, an average driver, of course, could not. The intensity at this pinnacle of stock car racing is among the highest in all sports.

A fraction of a second onto the time of the pole winner can send him home before the green flag falls. Side by side and nose to tail is the battle formation for four, five, or six hundred miles, and it is done 32 times a season.

From the sands along the shore at Daytona to the steep, sweeping turns of Talladega, through the serpentine turns of road courses and the tight confines of short tracks, generations of drivers have battled on the perilous edge of danger. Doing so they have thrilled fans and attracted the attention of the corporate giants of the nation.

Fast but close competitions have proven popular since the sanctioning body's first event nearly a half-century ago. From those formative years to the present day, NASCAR has afforded fans a varied selection of competition under their banner. As the racing giant nears its Golden Anniversary, the focus is on the highly popular Winston Cup Series. But there is also a large and growing following for NASCAR's other major touring divisions: The Busch and Busch North Series; Craftsman Trucks; Goody's Dash and Featherlite Modified Series, plus the small tracks throughout the country which host the weekly races for the Winston Racing Series.

On the following pages we will concentrate on the Winston Cup Series. We will look back at its history, where it came from and how it has grown to the unprecedented popularity of today. We will recall and examine some of the top teams in the sport's history to see when and why they were successful. We will give you a look-in at the sport's outstanding driving talents and the attributes which placed them so frequently in the victory lane. And we will look at some of the outstanding venues where this competition occurs, at the tracks which have been vital to the growth and expansion of NASCAR's elite formula of competition.

Each of these varied facets have contributed to the rocketing growth of the sport and its acceptance by both the nation's corporate community and the spectating public of the United States.

THE SKY'S THE LIMIT *As this grand old sport approaches its half-century things are looking up for NASCAR.*

THE HISTORY

FIRST AMONG EQUALS *Darlington was the first ever 500 mile race and is still a great challenge to any driver.*

TIM AND FONTY FLOCK *(pictured) were joined by their brother Bob and then their sister.*

The Florida sun shone shafts of brilliance into the large room atop the Daytona Beach hotel on a December day in 1947. Inside, cigar and cigarette smoke hung heavily in the air but there was no haze in the minds of the 35 men assembled.

Businessmen and moonshiners, race drivers, fast-talking promoters, and mechanics (some of them still showing trademark tinges of grease under their fingernails) composed themselves for the historic gathering.

The tall man who had called them together sat and explained the meeting's purpose. He requested the support, contributions, and suggestions of those assembled in forming an organization solely for the consolidation and enhancement of stock car racing.

'Big Bill' France, the six-foot-seven former driver and mechanic, had competed in and promoted stock car events in the Daytona area and throughout the Southeast since

moving to the area in the mid-1930s. He'd known success behind the wheel, and had seen the potential of the developing sport created by the nation's love affair with the automobile. Crucially, he gauged public interest in races between the kind of machines they drove, and knew that uniform rules, consistent technical standards, and assurances of advertised prize money being paid to the competitors were needed for the new sport to succeed. And a new benevolent fund for drivers 'laid up' by accidents would be created.

In post-war America, the public was looking for new and exciting recreational activities. Many had found this in the smattering of races held in the early post-war years as gasoline and tires became more available. But the events were haphazard, safety being largely ignored for contestants and public alike, and a diverse group of promoters were espousing their own racing circuits with claims of superiority and each

with a 'National Champion.' Bill France wanted to focus the fledgling sport, give it direction and have that direction take it to a national championship each season. The group agreed with the intent and the timeliness for such organization.

First, they needed a name. Among those suggested were National Championship Stock Car Circuit (NCSCC) and National Stock Car Racing Association (NSCRA). Then veteran Atlanta mechanic Red Vogt suggested they call it National Association of Stock Car Auto Racing and NASCAR came into being. The three-day meeting ironed out rules and regulations, by-laws, and guidelines for the group, which elected Bill France its first President and voted in other officers, including local driver Marshall Teague as the first Treasurer. Louis Ossinsky, a local attorney with offices across the street from France's gas station, was tapped to draw up the paper work. The task was completed February 21, 1948.

The new NASCAR organization ran its first race on Daytona's beach-road circuit six days before the papers were finalized and filed, but that event, won by Robert 'Red' Byron in Raymond Parks' 1939 Ford tuned by Louis 'Red' Vogt, marked the beginning of competition under the NASCAR banner. The beach race was the first of 52 events run that inaugural season. The winning team from the first event went on to become the initial champions of the organization.

A circuit for new cars—post-war models—had been planned for the 1948 campaign but never materialized. Cars were still scarce and the public didn't want to see a car they couldn't buy getting banged up in a race. But availability increased, and by 1949 cars were flowing into dealerships. France tried the idea again, first as part of an undercard at a track in southern Florida. The event was a moderate success, so France made plans for a new 'Strictly Stock' race that Spring on a three-quarter mile dirt oval in Charlotte, North Carolina, with a whopping purse of $5,000 on the line, $2,000 of that earmarked for the winner.

The response was immediate.

France had no problem filling the 33-car field and fans jammed the track. Bob Flock, the oldest of the three racing brothers, was the division's first pole winner with his youngest brother, Tim, starting second, and the middle sibling, Fonty, earning the fifth place for the start. The field even included a female driver, with Sarah Christian starting 13th in her husband's Ford. The race drew drivers from as far away as Kansas. That's where Jim Roper learned of it while reading the 'Smiling Jack' newspaper comic strip drawn by France's friend and race fan Zack Mosley, who put racing references into his drawings.

That first event was awarded to Roper after flagged winner Glenn Dunnaway became the circuit's first disqualification. His Ford was found to have 'altered rear springs' in the post-race inspection, a violation of the 'strictly stock' rules which allowed only reinforcement of the right front wheel. Although the first to the checkered flag (by a three-lap margin), Dunnaway was dropped to the bottom of the results table. Albeit three laps shy of running the full distance, Roper's Lincoln moved to the top of the list to become the first winner in NASCAR's new major league. Finishing second in that inaugural was Hudson-mounted Fonty Flock. Third went to Red Byron in an Olds 88, with fellow Olds drivers Sam Rice and Tim Flock rounding out the top five.

The huge crowd was thrilled by the racing, even though only one accident occurred during the race. That happened when Lee Petty flipped the family Buick to end his day. Perhaps more pleased than the fans was France himself. His idea had proved to be on target.

Quickly, seven more events were scheduled. They ran in Florida the next month, where the three Flocks were joined by their sister, Ethel, who was one of three distaff drivers in the race. Other races were held in New York, Pennsylvania, Virginia, and North Carolina with Byron driving the Vogt-tuned Parks' Olds to the division's initial championship.

In 1950 the circuit grew and the name changed to 'Grand National,' a title usually applied to major horse

BILL FRANCE JR *took over from Dad in 1972.*

races. Another major change happened that season as the circuit held their first race on a paved track and tried their first 500-mile race. Both occurred at Darlington (South Carolina) Speedway on the first Monday in September. The race was the 13th of that season's 19. No one was sure a stock car could last 500 miles, so 75 machines were allowed to try. Many couldn't go the distance but among those who did was Johnny Mantz in a Plymouth—he emerged the winner after more than six-and-a-half hours of racing. Super-Speedway racing had arrived.

In ensuing seasons the growth continued. By 1958, the division's tenth year, there were 51 races. The west coast was hosting some of them by then. The demand was so great that two races were often run on the same day, one on the east coast and the other out west.

The circuit grew to a high of 62 races in 1964 and other big tracks were built to host the events. Daytona's 2.5-mile track, opened in 1959, joined the next season alongside mile-and-a-half facilities in Charlotte, North Carolina, and Atlanta, Georgia. The one-mile track at Rockingham, North Carolina, came on board in 1965, followed by the addition of more tracks as the 1960s drew to a close. Dover, Delaware, Michigan International Speedway, and the 2.66-mile, 33-degree Talladega SuperSpeedway all entered the scene in 1969.

The growth was not trouble-free, despite France's organization. In the mid-1960s, the factory-backed teams boycotted the circuit in a dispute over rules. Participating tire companies warred with each other for supremacy in the sport. A national fuel shortage threatened to halt racing until France shortened all races by ten percent and had a study done to prove that auto racing in America used less fuel than most other sports.

A big step for the circuit came in 1971 when R. J. Reynolds Tobacco Company assumed sponsorship of the division. Lending their marketing acumen to the already thriving sport, a huge growth spurt followed as the series dropped to running just 30 races a season, all of them major events. The new, slimmer but more competitive division became known as the Winston Cup Series as it entered its 'Modern Era' of approximately 30 races per season in 1972.

Perhaps the biggest boost came with the 1979 running of the Daytona 500. It was the first of the division's events to be afforded live start-to-finish coverage by a major television network (CBS). A great race, on a day when much of the populous eastern half of the country was snowed in, attracted thousands of new fans, and many Fortune 500 companies sought involvement.

France stepped aside in 1972. He'd watched his concept come to fruition. The tall man with the ready smile and soft Southern accent turned the organization's reins over to his son Bill, who has mentored its steady growth ever since.

Today, under Bill France, Jr's guidance, every race carries posted awards in excess of $1 million, all Winston Cup races are shown live, flag-to-flag on television, and most tracks have waiting lists of ticket buyers wanting to watch the colorful—and heavily sponsored—cars compete.

The 35 men who met in that smoke-filled room in 1947 had clear foresight. What they created has become the largest attended, most lucrative and most competitive form of racing under the sun.

FAST CARS AND MONEY *Today NASCAR is big business and one of the greatest events America has to offer.*

EARNHARDT

THE GREAT

In every field of endeavor, there are individuals who stand head and shoulders above their peers. In stock car racing, that may be fender and hood ahead of their field.

He watched his father and learned how to race and win. Choosing to follow in his father's tire tracks, the young Earnhardt had to work on his own cars, but by doing so found how and why a race car worked.

He moved up to Winston Cup in 1975, making occasional starts while pursuing his short-track career. In 1979, he hooked up with owner Rod Osterlund and began a full-time major league career which would lead to that season's Rookie of The Year title and his first victory at Bristol, Tennessee. The 1980 campaign proved the prior season and title was no fluke as Earnhardt won five times and took the first of his seven Winston Cup championships. Since, he has won more than five dozen times in his relentless give-no-quarter driving style, learned from his days of watching his father and years of battling on short tracks.

Earnhardt, with career earnings rapidly nearing the $30 million mark (a world motorsports record), has won on super-speedways, intermediate tracks, short ovals and road courses. His resume also includes 23 triumphs in NASCAR's Busch Series, a trio in the annual all-star, winners-only 'The Winston,' six triumphs in the season-opening pole position-winners-only Busch Clash, a record nine wins in the Daytona 500's qualifying races, and a 1990 championship in the IROC Series.

In 1997, he began his 14th season as the driver of Chevrolets fielded by Richard Childress Racing.

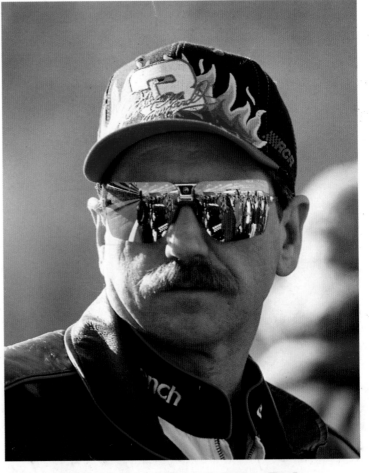

A second generation driver, Dale Earnhardt grew up following his racing champion father Ralph to the short ovals around the Southeastern quadrant of America.

DRIVERS

The following is a glance at some of the men, winners all, who have excelled (the order does not reflect any ranking.)

Tall, lanky, red-headed Bill Elliott emerged from his native north Georgia in 1976, after a career of racing on that area's dirt tracks with his brothers, Ernie and Dan, to try NASCAR's major league.

In his first race Elliot came a humbling 33rd. He didn't run the full schedule until 1983, the year he scored his first victory. It came in the season-ending Winston Western 500 on California's twisting Riverside road course, in his second season as driver of the potent Ford Thunderbirds for Michigan businessman Harry Melling. Their relationship would last ten seasons and enjoy far greater success.

1985 was the team's most prolific and rewarding season, as they set qualifying and race records unmatched in the next decade. The Elliott-Melling combo won 11 poles (including a NASCAR record 212.809 mph run at Talladega) and as many races, all on the circuit's big tracks, the latter a still standing single-season record. Included among that year's win came victories in the Daytona 500, Winston 500 (Talladega), and Darlington's famed Southern 500, to make him the winner of 'The Winston Million' in the first year the $1 million award was offered for any driver to win three or four selected major events (that quartet also includes Charlotte's World 600 race in May). Although offered annually since, Elliott stands as sole claimant.

Before forming his own team in 1995, Elliott spent three seasons (1992–1994) driving Fords for Junior Johnson. The pairing won four straight events following the 1992 Daytona 500 to equal the mark for most consecutive victories in the current climate of about 30 event seasons.

GORDON

Although just 24 years old when he won the 1995 Winston Cup crown, the talented youngster already had 19 years of racing experience.

Gordon's is a career that began in his native California, when he started racing quarter midget cars at the age of five. To enhance his talent and hone his skills, his family moved to Indiana eight years later where he quickly adapted to larger forms of machinery. In 1990 he earned the championship in the Midget Car division of the United States Auto Club, and the following year took the driving crown in the larger USAC Silver Crown Series, while also earning Rookie of the Year honors in NASCAR's Busch Series.

In 1993, just his second season in stock cars, Gordon won a series record 11 poles in the Busch Series and scored his first three victories under the NASCAR banner. That fall he was tapped by the team owner to drive a Winston Cup Chevrolet in the season-ending race at Atlanta.

Halfway through just his second full season in the big league of stock car competition, Gordon scored his first major victory in the 1994 World 600 at Charlotte, the circuit's longest event. That August, he added to his reputation by winning the inaugural running of the Brickyard 400 at Indianapolis Motor Speedway in the first event ever held at the storied facility and the richest event in the sport's history. Gordon's Indy winnings were a NASCAR event total $613,000. He had already scored

twice in the ultra-competitive environment with victories in his 1993 Daytona 500 qualifying race and in the 1994 Busch Clash. The latter started the season which led to his Rookie of the Year title.

Gordon added seven victories to his total in 1995 en route to the Championship, plus a victory in the Winston All-Star race and won season high ten races in the 1996 campaign, only to fall 37 points shy of a second straight title behind his Hendrick Motorsports teammate, Terry Labonte. He atoned for that deficit by winning the 1997 Daytona 500 as he led a one-two-three sweep of the event by the Hendrick Chevrolet trio—Gordon, Labonte, and Ricky Craven.

Robert Glen Johnson, Jr., known to family, friends and the world simply as Junior Johnson, is still recognized as one of the hardest chargers ever to grip a steering wheel.

JOHNSON

The sun-baked Wilkes County, North Carolina, native was relieved when his brother called him in from the field. Dropping the mule's reins, the stocky youth trudged through the broken red clay to learn the cause of his summons. He was pleased to be asked to drive his older brother's car in a fill-in 'Moonshiners' race between the regular Modified racing events at the local North Wilkesboro Speedway. Pulling on his boots, he quickly accepted, thinking it would sure beat plowing the field.

Thus began the career of Junior Johnson. By the time he moved to NASCAR big time in the l953 Southern 500 at Darlington, he had already earned nicknames like 'Wilkes County's Wild Man' and 'Ronda Road Runner' for his all-out driving style. He had a technique on the era's dirt tracks and mastery on pavement honed from years of out-running the Federal Revenue agents —'Revenooers'—while making deliveries from his father's stills that lay sequestered around the Blue Ridge section of North Carolina, surrounding the family's home in Ronda.

Johnson's initial victory came at the one-third mile Hickory Speedway in 1955. His last was recorded ten years later on his local North Wilkesboro tracks; it was the 50th of his career. Between those two triumphs had come wins at Daytona, Darlington, Charlotte, Martinsville, Bristol, Atlanta, and many other tracks.

When the North Wilkesboro track closed at the end of 1996, Johnson was still tied as the second most prolific pole winner in the facility's history, even though he hadn't raced there in 30 years.

It was his second straight win in the Charlotte's track that led him to retire, at age 35, in 1966. 'There warn't [sic] any special thrill in the second win. The first was special, 'cause I hadn't done it afore. I'd beat 'em everywhere we raced. Doin' it again just didn't mean that much to me,' Johnson explained.

A talented driver and top mechanic, Johnson is still ranked as one of the sport's top chauffeurs, even though he attained even greater success as a team owner after he last donned a helmet.

PETTY

'The King' of stock car racing was an awkward prince when he climbed into his father's back-up car to start his first big time race on a short track in Toronto, Canada, in 1958.

By the time he climbed out for the final time after the season-ending event in 1994 Richard Petty had earned his regal title by virtue of his record 200 victories, seven driving championships, and seven victories in the prestige-laden Daytona 500. His victory total is 95, more than his nearest rival, David Pearson, and a difference of 18 more than the number of wins by any other driver in the sport's history. (No driver, other than Petty and Pearson, has won 85 races.)

But more than winning, Richard Petty gained much of his acclaim by an off-track presence and willingness to carry himself as a champion and representative of his sport. At a White House reception in Washington or a business convention in Chicago, Petty was the essence of a professional stock car driver. Even more important was his pioneering relationship with race fans. Win or lose, elated or disappointed, Petty was never too busy to sign every autograph requested. He would visit terminally ill youngsters, call shut-ins, joke with pit visitors, and always sold his sport.

Among his innumerable records, the 1967 season stands out. In his 48 starts that season, he wound up in victory lane an incredible 27 times, including a summer-to-fall run of ten consecutive wins. His 1959 Rookie of the Year title didn't come close to indicating future success.

Before he retired, the second generation stock car racer won on every type of track the sport offered— short-dirt ovals, road courses, intermediate speedways, paved short tracks, and super-speedways. His 200th and final win came at Daytona Speedway, with the President of the United States, Ronald Reagan, in attendance on July 4, 1984.

Over his 35-year driving career, Petty started a record 1,177 races with 549 top five finishes. He was voted Most Popular driver nine times. His career began as a lad battling fender-to-fender with the sport's pioneers, and he ended it racing their sons and grandsons, plus a bevy of new drivers who grew up hearing of the talent and legend of Richard Petty. He is still on the scene with his trademark cowboy hat, flowing mustache, and dazzling smile, but now his role is as car owner.

Edward Glenn Roberts, Jr., was born and grew up in Florida. His prowess as a high school baseball pitcher earned him the nickname 'Fireball'

ROBERTS

He carried the Fireball nickname throughout his career in racing, although he didn't care for it personally. He was known to family and close friends as Glenn. When racing resumed after World War II, it attracted the 18-year-old, who made his initial start in his Daytona Beach home town in the August 1947 race on the famed beach road circuit. He drove a modified Ford to a respectable seventh place finish. The tall, athletically-built Roberts scored his first major league victory three years later in a 100-mile chase on the mile, dirt oval at Hillsborough, North Carolina. It would be an omen of future success on the circuits and major tracks which lay in the future of the sport.

In 1957, he was the first winner of a Convertible race at the famed Darlington track in South Carolina, a difficult facility where he would triumph three more times. He was also pole and race winner of the 1.5-mile Atlanta track when it opened in 1960 and the top qualifier at Charlotte's Motor Speedway's first two events, also in 1960.

But it was on his home town track, Daytona International Speedway (which replaced the beach road circuit in 1959) where Roberts was allowed to display his skill and daring. The crew-cut blond speedster was the 2.5-mile track's top qualifier in five of the first major stock car races, and in 1962 was the first to take pole honors, win the qualifying race and win the Daytona 500. He

returned that Summer to take the 250-mile race and became the first driver to score a sweep of the track's two major events in a single season. His 250 win that summer was his third in the event's first five editions.

Roberts' 33rd and final triumph came in November 1963 on a three-mile road course in Augusta, Georgia. He suffered fatal burns in a wreck in Charlotte's World 600 in May 1964 and died July 2. His passing ended the career of the first professional race driver his sport had seen.

Roberts was a pro to his peers, the media, and the public. He left his sport a legacy of skill, determination, and physical presence. He was smooth and glib with the media, cordial and friendly with fans, and a joy to watch on a race track.

STOCK CAR RACERS

There is only a slight difference between the great drivers and those who are outstanding. Some of the following individuals might well be included in the first category. Each certainly were and are important to racing's growth, and outstanding in skill, significance and contribution to the sport and business of stock car racing.

BOBBY ALLISON *A force to be reckoned with, throughout his 22 racing years.*

Bobby Allison

A native of southern Florida but Alabamaian by choice, Robert Arthur 'Bobby' Allison grew up watching the racing in the Miami area. Too small for the traditional school sports, he migrated to motorsports as an equalizer. Honing his skills on the Florida tracks in 'jalopy' races, he moved up to the Modified division of NASCAR, winning two national championships and two 'Special Modified' titles before going into Winston Cup full-time in the mid-1960s.

In the big league of stock car racing he won 84 times in 717 starts and claimed the Winston Cup crown in 1983. His driving career ended with a near fatal wreck at Pocono in 1988, but found him driving (and winning) for every factory during the 22-year span of full-time competition.

Red Byron

A wounded World War II flier, Robert 'Red' Byron resumed his post-war racing career by winning. The Alabama driver was the winner of NASCAR's first race (February 1948) and went on to win the first championship offered under its banner. Byron, who had to strap his shrapnel-wounded leg in order to drive, would be the first champion of what has become the Winston Cup Series.

Although running only briefly in those events, Byron won just twice in 14 starts, but forged a dozen top ten finishes, eight in the top five positions, while taking three titles in the faster Modified Division.

While others won more, Byron will always be NASCAR's first winner. When a heart attack took his life in 1960, he was manager of a team preparing for the first 24-hour Daytona.

Tim Flock

The youngest of the three Hall of Fame racing brothers, Julius Timothy Flock had the most outstanding record. A two-time Champion and 40-race winner in the sport's big league, the Alabama native was among the smoothest and most consistent of the sport's pioneers. He won five times on Daytona's famed beach road circuit, considered the toughest on man and machine in those early years. He had two more victories on that course which were disallowed due to minor technical discrepancies.

Flock's best season came at the wheel of the potent Carl Riekhaefer Chrysler 300s in 1955, when he won 18 races, was top qualifier 19 times, and boasted 32 top five finishes in 38 starts.

In 187 Winston Cup events (1949–61), Flock had 129 top ten finishes, completed over 85 percent of his possible laps and led nearly a quarter of the laps he ran. Smooth and steady, Flock took care of his equipment as shown by running at the finish of three quarters of his races.

Ned Jarrett

'Gentleman Ned' won his first race car in a poker game. Having tinkered with racing while working at the family sawmill, his advocation became a trade when he entered his newly-won mount in the 1953 Southern 500 at Darlington. He finished last in that outing but by the time he drove his last race at Rockingham, North Carolina, 13 years later with a third place finish, his record boasted 50 victories and two driving championships.

Jarrett's first title (1960) led him to take a public speaking course to enhance his role as NASCAR Champion and fulfill the speaking engagements resulting from that fame. His second crown in 1965 led him to enroll his entire crew in the same program.

In his second title season, Jarrett drove to 13 victories and had an equal number of second places in 54 starts. Included in that year's triumphs was a win in the same Southern 500 where he'd made that first start.

Retiring at 34 years of age, Jarrett had gone on to a highly respected career as an analyst for television coverage of his sport on ESPN and CBS, further utilizing the skills he decided to learn as a stock car champion.

NED JARRETT *He took a public speaking course in 1960 which stood him in good stead for his post-racing career.*

Terry Labonte

Titled 'The Ice Man' because of his cool demeanor, the Texas native began his racing career driving quarter midgets around the Corpus Christi area as a child. Graduating to late model stocks as a teen, Terry became the scourge of dirt and paved Texas short tracks before making his first stab at NASCAR's big time with a start in 1990 at Darlington. Although considered by most as the hardest Winston Cup track to drive, he surprised many, including himself, with a fourth place finish in the race he would win two years later.

Four years later, 'Texas Terry' won the first of his two Winston Cup championships through smooth driving and consistent finishes. En route to his second title (1996), Labonte earned another label. This one was 'Iron Man,' as he started his 514th consecutive race breaking the mark previously set by Richard Petty at 513. Well into the 1997 season, Labonte continues to add to his longevity, despite driving the last two 1996 events with a broken hand.

Through the campaign of 1996, Labonte's record showed 18 victories in 542 races plus 158 top five finishes and 47 front-row starts as he continues to quietly show his driving skills.

David Pearson

Raised in a poor textile village in South Carolina, Pearson found escape in racing. He started on the dirt ovals as a youth but found his greatest success on the big tracks of NASCAR's Winston Cup Series. A stealthy driver, he earned the title 'Silver Fox' as much for his prematurely grey hair as for his slyness on the track.

The winner of 105 races, second only to Richard Petty's 200, Pearson won the Winston Cup crown three times during a career which saw him master Darlington, Charlotte, Atlanta, and Daytona.

Following his 1960 Rookie of the Year season, Pearson won three big track races in 1961 and became the first to win more than two in a year as he scored victories at Charlotte, Daytona, and Atlanta.

Driving the red-and-white Purolator Mercury for the Wood brothers in 1976, Pearson enjoyed his best season. Running an abbreviated schedule of 22 (of 30) races, he won ten times and had six more top four finishes while making 13 front row starts.

Lee Petty

The patriarch of a racing family that has seen three generations victorious in the intense competition of NASCAR's biggest circuit, Lee Arnold Petty had an ignoble start. He drove the family Buick from their home in Randleman, North Carolina, to compete in the 1949 inaugural 'Strictly Stock' (nee Winston Cup) race at Charlotte. He was one of the starters and the only one to flip his car during the race. Despite that he finished second in that first season's point chase (behind only Byron) and went on to win the coveted title three times before a 1961 wreck at Daytona cut short his career.

Even though his driving days ended there, the 2.5 mile track was also the location of his biggest victory. When the track opened in 1959, Petty drove his Oldsmobile to victory in the inaugural Daytona 500 in a photo finish with Iowa's Johnny Beauchamp.

Although it was just one of his career's 54 victories, it was one on which careers are judged. Lee Petty's was judged to be great, as he scored 321 top ten finishes in 429 starts.

Marshall Teague

An Air Force flight engineer in Asia during World War II, Marshall Teague returned to his native Daytona Beach to take up a racing career he had dreamed of while overseas. He had seen some of the early beach races while growing up and got the chance to compete in them when racing resumed in 1946.

Teague won the big race on the beach in 1951. NASCAR had to phone the car's specifications for the post-race inspection. Thus the manufacturer learned one of their cars had won a big stock car race and invited Teague and his wife to visit. So impressed were the Hudson executives, they agreed to supply Teague with cars and parts to continue his racing. Local newspapers wrote about the Pure Oil gas station owner who created the first factory car deal and the Pure officials also feted the Teagues. During that visit, Marshall convinced them supplying products for the racers was good for business.

The 1952 beach races found Teague driving his factory Hudson Hornet to victory again, second place going to Herb Thomas in Teague's second Hornet. Both used pure products. Later in 1952, Teague drove his Hornet past 46 cars in the first dozen laps to lead the Southern 500 at Darlington. Thomas went on to win the race in the other Teaguemobile.

Elected the original Treasurer, Teague later switched his alliance to AAA to race at Indianapolis, but not before winning seven times under the NASCAR banner. He died in an Indy car crash while testing at the new Daytona Speedway in 1959.

LEE PETTY'S *His racing family seldom overshadows what was a remarkable career, with an inauspicious beginning.*

Herb Thomas

One of NASCAR's original super stars, Herb Thomas was the first repeat champion of NASCAR's biggest division. A tobacco farmer in his native North Carolina when not gripping the controls of a race car, Thomas won the new car circuit's title in 1951 and repeated the victory two years later.

At a time when Darlington was the only big track on the circuit and the Labor Day event there its only 500-mile race, Thomas became not just the first two-time winner, but the first to score three times in the then unique but still prestigious event. He won 1951's second running and then became the first back-to-back winner by scoring again in the 1954 and 1955 editions, winning each time for a different car owner.

In the end Thomas' career spanned 48 victories over eight seasons. It was cut short when he was severely injured in the third-from-final event of the 1956 season while leading the point standings. He tried two more events but announced his retirement in September 1957 at the same Shelby, North Carolina, dirt track where he had been injured a year earlier.

Rusty Wallace

In 1980 at Atlanta, Rusty Wallace drove a Roger Penske Chevrolet to second place in the Atlanta 500. It raised some eyebrows, coming in the Missourian's first start in NASCAR's big time. Those brows would not have been so high if their owners had checked the redhead's credentials: USAC Stock Car 1979 Rookie of the Year and son of a three-time track champion in his native St Louis.

The eldest of the three racing brothers concentrated on events in the Midwest for the next three seasons, winning frequently and gaining the 1983 American Speed Association (ASA) championship. He returned to take NASCAR Rookie honors in 1984 to start a career that carried him to 46 wins over the next dozen seasons and the 1989 Winston Cup championship. (He was first runner-up for that honor two other times, losing out by just 24 points to Dale Earnhardt in 1993.)

A terror on both short tracks and road courses, Wallace scored 25 victories in the 1993 through 1996 seasons and was 1991 champion of the International Race of Champions (IROC) Series.

HERB THOMAS *One of NASCAR's first super stars but his career was curtailed due to a severe accident.*

Darrell Waltrip

A three-time Winston Cup champion since the start of his major league career at Talladega, Alabama, in 1972, Darrell Waltrip has become the sport's elder statesman. Quick witted and silver tongued, Waltrip came out of Owensboro, Kentucky, as a short track demon. Moving to the Nashville suburb of Franklin to pursue racing at the Tennessee Fairgrounds' oval, Waltrip honed his skills in racing and the quip as he won the track's driving title.

The 1981, 1982, and 1985 Winston Cup champion was the inaugural winner of The Winston All-Star, winners-only race in 1985 at Charlotte Motor Speedway. His 84 career wins tie him with Bobby Allison for third on the sport's all-time list. His count includes a record dozen wins—including seven consecutive—on the high banks at Bristol, Tennessee. In his first two championship campaigns Waltrip won a dozen each season, driving cars fielded by the legendary Junior Johnson among the 43 won in their six years together.

Waltrip is the only five-time winner of Charlotte's 600-miler, the longest event of the season, a 13-time winner in NASCAR's Busch Series, the first three-time honoree as American Driver of the Year, and a five-time winner at the venerable egg-shaped Darlington oval.

Cale Yarborough

The stocky South Carolinian learned hard work as he grew up on the small family farm. It was this work ethic which led William Caleb Yarborough to 83 Winston Cup wins in 559 starts over a 26-year career. It is a span which found him the only driver in the sport's history to win three consecutive championships.

From sneaking, underage, under the fence to race at Darlington near his boyhood home, to becoming the first five-time winner of the track's famed Southern 500, Yarborough climbed the ladder of racing. His eight Daytona wins rank him second only to Richard Petty. He also won seven times at Atlanta, a trio at Charlotte, and nine times at Bristol, and was the inaugural NASCAR winner at Michigan International Speedway. He was the first to top 200 mph in qualifying at Daytona (1984) and exceeded that mark by a NASCAR record 15 times. His 70 career poles include a series record 14 during the 1980 campaign, his last of nine driving for Junior Johnson.

Yarborough retired as a driver in 1988 but is still on the circuit as a team owner.

ELDER STATESMAN *Darrell Waltrip's wins have earned him a place in the records books and his personality a place in the fans' hearts.*

THE RACE

No driver can race without a car. Nor can they compete without the backing, preparation, and service of a talented crew headed by a leader. Over its history, the major NASCAR circuit has had many outstanding teams who had the right combination of those traits to be truly successful. In this section, we look at a few of the truly great teams in the history of the sport which were not only successful in winning races and championships, but were also innovative and contributed to the sport in which they participated.

DePaolo Engineering

In 1956, Ford Motor Company determined it would get serious about stock car racing. To do so, they named 1925 Indianapolis 500 winner Peter DePaolo to head their program under a DePaolo Engineering name plate. The stocky, mustachioed Italian selected Ralph Moody and Fireball Roberts as his drivers.

The team's first appearance came in the February race on the beach-road circuit in Daytona, with Moody bringing his motor home in third but Roberts dropping out with mechanical woes. It was a small start but built to success as Roberts won five times and Moody contributed four more wins in the initial season that saw West Coast stars Bill Amick and Bill Carden added to the stable, and had Joe Weatherly and Curtis Turner competing in the Convertible division. Turner put DePaolo's topless

Ford in victory lane 22 times in their 57-race campaign, while Weatherly added four victories.

In 1957, DePaolo added Marvin Panch and Ralph Earnhardt to the team now overseen by John Holman, a gravel-voiced mechanic with a keen business acumen. The team was even stronger as the new season opened. Panch won the first two races and the team, led by Roberts, swept the top four spots in the third. It was a feat they would repeat again at North Wilkesboro and remains unmatched by an owner. Turner, Weatherly and Roberts won 14 of the opening 21 Convertible events. Moody, Panch, Roberts, and new driver Paul Goldsmith won ten of the season's first 16 Grand National races before the bottom dropped out.

In early June 1957, all the factories got out of racing, Ford included. They gave the drivers a race car, tow truck, and tools. Moody hocked his airplane to buy the surplus parts and equipment, coupling with Holman to form an even more successful team.

Holman and Moody cars featured

a driver list reading like a Stock Car Hall of Fame roster: Roberts, Weatherly, Turner, Fred Lorenzen, Nelson Stacy, David Pearson, and Bobby Allison won 57 races at tracks on the Winston Cup circuit and a dozen more on tracks which stood where shopping malls now exist. Pearson won the driving crown for them in 1968 and 1969, with 27 victories over the two seasons.

The famed H-M logo faded from the scene as they quit fielding teams when the sport entered the 1970s, but the legacy of the organization and excellence they represented impacts the teams of the 1990s.

Hendrick Motorsports

In 1984, a car dealer and former boat drag racer named Rick Hendrick decided he wanted to go stock car racing in NASCAR's major league. He hired veteran

crew chief Harry Hyde to build his team and tagged modified standout and Late Model winner Geoff Bodine to be his driver. The team came together quickly as they won their eighth start together at Martinsville, Virginia. That victory marked the emergence of Hendrick Motorsports.

The task wasn't easy. They had to beat the established and successful teams to succeed: groups like Junior Johnson's stable, the Fords of Bud Moore and Harry Melling, and fellow Chevy owner Richard Childress.

By the 1986 campaign, Hendrick was fielding a two-car team with Bodine and brash newcomer Tim Richmond behind the wheels, while expanding his shops and adding mechanical talent. They won nine of the year's 29 events. By 1987, Hendrick was sending as many as five cars to races. Star drivers Darrell Waltrip and Benny Parsons were seated in the Hendrick mounts and everyone knew the talented teams would have to be reckoned with. Hendrick built his racing organiza-

TEAMS

tion with the same skills he had utilized to bring his far flung dealerships to prominence in the country: through acute business senses, attracting talented people, and strong sponsorship support.

Quick to recognize talent and with 32 victories to his credit by the end of the 1992 campaign, Hendrick was able to lure sprint car and midget ace Jeff Gordon out of the Busch Series ranks and away from the Ford camp and into his Chevrolets. Gordon quickly became a winner and by 1995 was Hendrick's first Winston Cup Champion. It was a thrill Hendrick felt again in 1996 as Terry Labonte took the crown in a season-ending battle between Labonte and Gordon. It marked only the second time in the sport's history any owner has won consecutive titles with different drivers and the first time it had happened in nearly forty seasons.

The Hendrick Motorsports teams won 22 of the 62 races during the 1995–1996 seasons, a dominant number, through shared technology and skilled personnel on both sides of the pit wall and in their three shops. In four of the 1996 events, Hendrick cars finished one-two.

Although diagnosed with a rare bone marrow cancer after the 1996 season, Hendrick had his biggest thrill in the 1997 season-opening Daytona 500, as he watched his trio of cars take the top three spots in the nationally televized event. Gordon, Labonte and former Rookie of the Year Ricky Craven brought the Hendrick Chevrolets home in the same event where his team owner's career had begun 13 seasons earlier and lifted him above the five-dozen victory level.

DePaolo *had success with the team of Ralph Moody (middle) and John Holmes (left) who carried the torch when Ford pulled out.*

Junior Johnson & Associates

Junior Johnson's Hall of Fame driving career ended when he last doffed his helmet at the end of the 1966 season. It was then he donned his car owner's headgear. In doing so, the portly North Carolina native began an equally storied career in the major league of American stock car racing.

His car, with Darell Dieringer driving, convincingly won the first year out. At Johnson's home track, North Wilkesboro, Dieringer earned the pole position and proceeded to lead all 400 laps of the race. A few years later, Johnson's car did the same, with Cale Yarborough now in the seat, at Bristol, Tennessee, where he commanded the field for all 500 circuits. It is the only time any driver led every lap on any of the tracks which have been part of the sport's modern era.

Between the two events' domination, Johnson cars were equally stout. In 1969, with LeeRoy Yarborough driving, the team won the Daytona 500, Charlotte's World 600, and Darlington's Southern 500—the biggest, longest, and oldest events on the big track schedule. The same feat today would have earned them the 'Winston $Million' and something done just three times over the events' histories.

A great era for Johnson's teams came in the 1970s when Cale Yarborough handled the driving duties. It was an era which saw them win 55 races, 39 poles, and three consecutive (1976–78) Winston Cup championships, the latter a feat not duplicated before or since. Johnson teamed with Charlotte Motor Speedway head Richard Howard in 1971 to bring a competitive Chevrolet back to the circuit. They succeeded by winning the pole for Charlotte's 600-miler and winning the fastest race in the history of Bristol's oval, both with 'Chargin' Charlie Glotzbach as driver.

The following year, the Howard-owned, Johnson-managed Chevy had Bobby Allison driving to ten wins in 31 starts, with a dozen more second place finishes. They started on the front row in 19 of those races, including 11 pole positions. They were the car to beat as they led the first 30 races of that 1971 season's 30 events.

Wishing to reduce his schedule, Yarborough left Johnson and was quickly succeeded by a brash youngster from Tennessee named Darrell Waltrip. Displaying the powerful potential of the team, they won a dozen races in each of their first two seasons together and took back-to-back championships for their efforts. They were still teamed in 1985 when The Winston All-Star race was first run. They were the inaugural winners and went on to win the World 600 the next day. That big weekend came in the midst of a super season by Bill Elliott, when he drove Harry Melling's Ford to the Winston $Million pay day for winning three of the circuit's big four events. But, at season's end, it was Johnson's car with Waltrip driving that won the 1985 championship, their third together.

As a car owner, Johnson had watched stoically as his vehicles won 139 times and earned six championships. But to the former moonshiner, it was no fun anymore. He retired again at the end of the '96 campaign, leaving the sport richer by his presence and with a record of success seldom found.

LEFT: *Hendrick Motorsports dominated 1996 and* **ABOVE:** *Junior Johnson had his first win as owner in 1967.*

CARL KIEKHAEFER *Pictured with the Flock brothers. The innovative businessman was so successful that he had to pull out of the sport.*

Carl Kiekhaefer

Obstinate, cantankerous, opinionated, tyrannical, peculiar, and dictatorial are words used to describe Carl Kiekhaefer of Fond Du Lac, Wisconsin's millionaire owner of Mercury Outboard Motors, who emerged on the stock car scene suddenly at the start of the 1955 season. Another term often assigned to his business and racing efforts is 'successful.' He was all of those, as well as being an innovator.

When NASCAR's major league arrived at the Daytona beach road course for the first big event of their 1955 campaign, they faced a new entry. A gleaming Chrysler 300 with 'Mercury Outboards' emblazoned on its sides. No driver had been named to the mount but

KIekhaefer quickly signed Tim Flock, who had won the race a year earlier but quit NASCAR after being disqualified for a minor rules violation. The team clicked immediately. Flock drove 'Mr K's' big white car to 18 poles and an equal number of race wins (both thought unbeatable at the time) and the 1955 Series championship.

The Mercury team out-factoried the factories, first adding a second car driven by Tim's brother Fonty, and then a third with Alfred 'Speedy' Thompson behind the wheel. Each team had its own truck to transport it to the races in an era when most were driven or towed from race to race. Each crew of mechanics had uniforms, a bit of showmanship and professionalism unprecedented a the time. The irascible owner hired a hi-sown meteorologist to record weather factors and a geologist to sample and test the dirt of racing surfaces.

Kiekhaefer let no stone unturned in his drive to not only win but to dominate the sport. His cars won 22 of the 40 races they entered in 1955 with one-two finishes in four. In 11 of his 18 victories that season Tim Flock led every lap. For a 300 mile race at the 1.5-mile Le-Hi Speedway in West Memphis, Arkansas, Kiekhaefer entered four cars. All three Flock brothers—Tim, Fonty, and Bob—drove, plus AAA talent Norm Nelson, and he sponsored the other top contenders, even Ford factory teams from DePaolo Engineering. Speedy Thompson drove one of the latter to victory carrying the Mercury Outboard logo.

If the competition thought 1955 had been good for the 'K' cars, they hadn't seen anything. He came to Daytona in 1956 with a five-car effort, having hired Buck Baker, Frank 'Rebel' Mundy and Charlie Scott (only the second

Afro-American in the sport) to complement Tim Flock and Thompson. Flock gave him a second straight beach victory. His cars won 21 of the season's first 25 races. Flock suffered from ulcers and quit the team only to be replaced by Herb Thomas. The teams took 16 races in a row from March into May. Baker won 14 events that season and gave Kiekhaefer his second consecutive title, the first time in the sport's history anyone won straight owner titles with different drivers.

As suddenly as he had arrived, Kiekhaefer was gone. His frequent wins and domination of the sport resulted in boos of resentment from the fans. Fearing a negative effect on Mercury Outboard motor sales, the millionaire closed his racing shop and didn't return to a track until he was inducted into the sport's Hall of Fame at Darlington in 1980.

Petty Enterprises

To the inaugural 'Strictly Stock' at Charlotte in 1949, a farmer from central North Carolina brought the family Buick. He returned home chagrined. He had wrecked the car, rolling it in the race—the event's only mishap. His wife was not pleased with the results but Lee Petty was not deterred.

The incident was the start of a racing operation which has been the most successful in the history of the sport that became today's Winston Cup Series. Petty ran five more of the first season's races and would up second in the standings at season's end only to champion Red Byron. All five of Petty's starts after the Charlotte debacle resulted in top ten finishes, including a win at Heidelburg Speedway in Pittsburgh. He thus established a pattern of success through consistent performance that became the foundation for Petty Enterprises.

Lee Petty's career launched a racing operation which has earned an unprecedented ten championships in NASCAR's major circuit and recorded an unmatched 269 victories over the next 49 seasons. Included among the latter total are an enviable nine Daytona 500 victo-ries, and the drivers who have won for the team are a Hall of Fame group. The latest addition to the list came from Bobby Hamilton's victory in 1996 at Phoenix to mark the fourth decade that has seen a Petty entry in victory lane.

The family store launched the career of Lee's son Richard toward his status as 'The King of Stock Car Racing.' It is a title earned by his 200 wins, seven driving crowns, and his seven visits to the Daytona 500 winners' circle where Lee Petty was the inaugural honoree in following the event's initial running in 1959. It was under the Petty banner that Richard raced in the 1967 season when he set the single-season record of 27 victories, including ten consecutive, which is the only streak to exceed the mark set by Tim Flock in the Kiekhaefer Chryslers a dozen seasons earlier.

Before being severely injured in a Daytona 500 qualifying race in 1961, Lee had amassed 54 victories and three driving crowns. He was the series' first three-time champion, and might have earned it many more times but for being stripped of points a couple of seasons for competing in non-NASCAR races.

Other major races won by Petty machines included the 1964 600 at Charlotte, when Jim Paschal drove the team's second entry, and Marvin Panch's triumph in the same event two seasons later. Pete Hamilton won the 1970 Daytona 500 for Petty Enterprises and went on to sweep both of that season's events at the new Talladega Super Speedway in Alabama. The Petty cars, with Richard Plymouth-mounted and Buddy Baker in the team's Dodge, finished one-two in the 1971 Daytona 500, with Baker going on to give the organization yet a third victory in Charlotte's grueling 600-miler.

Lee Petty retired following his 1961 injuries. Richard hung up his helmet following the final event of the 1992 campaign. But Petty Enterprises continues as a long-lived and integral part of NASCAR big time circuits. Kyle Petty—Richard's son, Lee's grandson—races out of the team's shop, along with Hamilton, some four dozen seasons after the family car was flipped upside-down.

PETTY ENTERPRISES *hold the top honors in the Winston Cup Series.*

Raymond Parks

Even before NASCAR was formed in 1948, the cars of Atlanta's Raymond Parks were winners. Tall, thin, and dapper under his ever-present full-brimmed hat, Parks fielded the best teams in the fledgling days of stock car racing. He hired the best drivers, top mechanics, and gave them whatever it took to produce winning efforts on the dirt tracks of those early years.

Five races were held on the early beach-road circuit in Daytona in the two years after World War II. Parks' cars won all of them. His drivers included Roy Hall, Rob Flock, and Red Byron during that period of 1946–47.

Parks was part of the meeting in December 1947. His chief mechanic, Red Vogt, was there, too, and proposed the name for the organization —NASCAR.

The new sanctioning body held its first race the next February on the hard-packed sands of Daytona. It was won by Byron in a car owned by Parks and prepared by Vogt. The team would go on to win the first championship under the organization's banner.

When NASCAR started its new car division in 1949, Parks' cars, prepared by Vogt and driven by Byron, were there. Although winning just twice, they finished well enough in the others to take the first championship for the Strictly Stock division which would become 'Grand National' the next season and grow to be today's Winston Cup Series.

While Byron was on his way to the inaugural crown for the new cars, Fonty Flock was busy winning the second straight Modified title in Parks' 1939 Ford. His success made him the first three-time championship owner and the only person of the sport's early era to win the titles of two NASCAR divisions in the same season.

The other victory Byron enjoyed in that precedent-setting 1949 campaign was his three-lap margin over Lee Petty in the circuit's inaugural event at Martinsville, Virginia's half-mile dirt oval. The triumph by Parks' Oldmobile began a skein augmented by Jeff Gordon's win on the same track in April 1997 to extend the longest run of continuous racing in NASCAR major league.

The growth of the sport in those early days led to Parks' departure. The expanded circuits were taking his time from the Parks' Novelty Company he ran in Atlanta. His vending machines needed his attention—they were what had provided his financial ability to field cars and support the sport. He is rumored to even have bankrolled a young race promoter named Bill France during some of the financially thin moments in the sport's infancy.

Parks left the sport with a legacy of class, some nice trophies, and a room full of memories he maintains in his Atlanta offices four decades after his significant contributions.

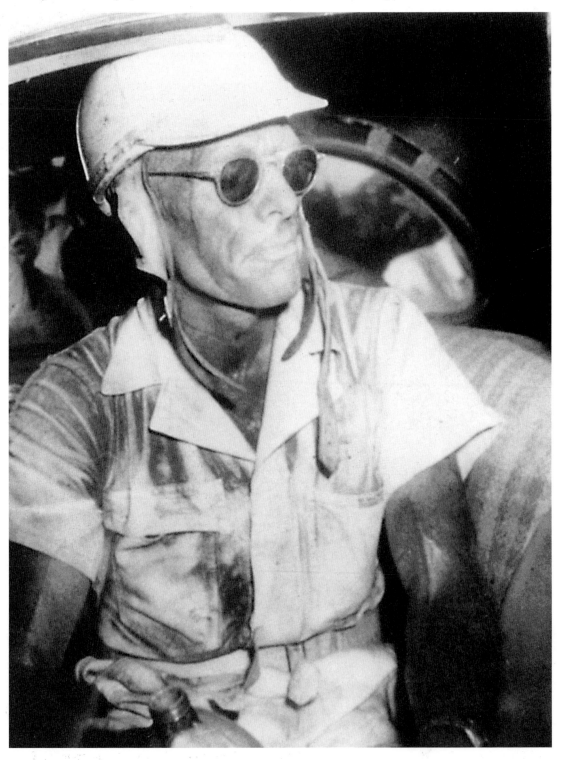

CLOSE TIES *NASCAR was named by Raymond Parks' chief mechanic and first won by his driver Red Byron, above.*

RICHARD CHILDRESS *has earned $27 million through Dale Earnhardt's hard work and a pit crew that won the Unocal/Rockingham competition for four straight years.*

Richard Childress Racing

The route to heading a successful team takes many paths. For Richard Childress it started by selling peanuts, as a kid, at the Bowman-Grey Stadium track in his native Winston Salem, North Carolina. He watched the local stars battle in modified cars and thrilled when NASCAR's major drivers came to race on the eight-quarter-mile oval twice a year. Before long he was tinkering on cars at local shops, then driving on the track which circled the stadium's football field.

His skills honed, he moved into the big time of stock car racing in 1972 as owner/driver with only childhood friend Tim Brewer to help. They raced for seven years and developed into one of the top independent teams before deciding Childress' best talent lay in organizing the operation. During his struggling effort, he gradually built his team in the image of the highly successful pattern established by his childhood hero, Junior Johnson.

With the days of successful independent teams rapidly fading, in mid-1981 Childress tapped another promising youngster who had also grown up in racing, Dale Earnhardt. Together they ran the final 11 events of the campaign, but at season's end Earnhardt was lured to the factory-aided Bud Moore team. Childress saw promise in Moore's driver, Ricky Rudd, and signed him as his driver for the next two seasons.

The combo tasted their first victory at Riverside (California) Raceway in June, 1983. They won again that Fall at Martinsville, Virginia. Childress found the success he'd hoped for. Moore and Childress exchanged drivers again following the 1983 campaign.

With Earnhardt in the car and Childress calling the shots, the success came quickly with wins at the huge Talladega track in Alabama and on the demanding mile and a half Atlanta oval. They have stayed to win races every season since.

Well staffed, equipped, and sponsored, the Richard Childress Racing company became the team to beat in every race and for every championship. The latter is a goal they have achieved six times in the 1980s and 90s. Each time the crowns of champion driver and owner have come back-to-back. They took their first title together in 1986 and repeated the next season. They were the best in the sport again in 1990 and 1991 and again in 1993 and 1994.

During the course of their association, they have won over 60 races. And while Earnhardt has left his moniker all over the champions' and all-time winners' tables but part of this success has come from fast and efficient pit work by Childress' staff. His is the only team to win the annual Unocal/Rockingham World Championship Pit Crew competition four straight years (1985–88). The team has also been dominant in the special all-star Busch Clash and Winston races. They have won the Clash, only open to the prior season's top qualifiers, a record five times, and have teamed to take 'The Winston' winners-only chase an unprecedented three times.

Richard Childress Racing, with Earnhardt in the driving seat, has earned over $27 million in competition. That's not small potatoes for a man who began his racing career selling peanuts.

49

THE RACE

There have been a variety of facilities which have hosted NASCAR's big time circuit, the Winston Cup Series. They have been as short as one-fifth of a mile and as long as 4.2 miles. They have been dirt and paved, flat and high banked. Each has had its own personality and degree of difficulty to the participants. This section takes a look at some of the prominent tracks and what makes them distinctively different.

Charlotte Motor Speedway

From near financial ruin to status as a showcase for stock car racing is the gamut run by the mile-and-a-half of asphalt known as Charlotte Motor Speedway. From the time co-founders Curtis Turner and Bruton Smith agreed to build it in 1959 until its emergence as one of the top tracks in NASCAR, the path has been a roller coaster journey.

From ground breaking in July 1959 until the first race the following June, work was frantic. Under-financed (as were many such endeavors of that era) and delayed by weather and geology, the construction progressed. Even the concept for the opening event was questioned. Rather than another 500-mile race like Darlington and Daytona offered, Turner and Smith decided to afford fans the longest race of the year to provide premiums not only on speed but durability as well. They thought of a 501-mile race with the checkered flag falling on the back stretch but discarded the concept in favor of a 600-miler. It would be something untried in the sport's annals.

Construction continued right into the opening time trials, as great quantities of rock were encountered where the farm field was thought to be only dirt. The untested paving did not stand up to the pounding of the cars. The race teams put deflectors on their hoods to protect the windshields from flying asphalt, and hung wire grates on the front of the cars to shield radiators, but the race ran.

Five dozen cars, aligned three abreast, took the starting flag. Less than a third of them were still racing at the end. Among the sidelined was Jack Smith, who had built a five-lap lead only to have an errant chuck of pavement punch a gaping hole in his Pontiac's fuel tank. Futile efforts were made at repairs as unsung Joe Lee Johnson made up the deficit and took command for the final 48 laps. He was first under the checkered flag, five-and-a-half hours after the start.

A smaller than expected crowd led to the track's reorganization under Federal Bankruptcy laws. It survived and has grown to become a pioneer facility in racing. Now luxurious corporate suites overlook the track, as do condominiums. Seating of over 100,000 would swallow the 35,000 who saw the first event and the 600s now take less than four hours to complete. The May classic is now one of

GROUND BEEF *Charlotte's rough surface caused many an upset on it's opening race.*

the four major events which count toward The Winston $Million and is still the longest distance event of each NASCAR season.

Durability has also improved through the intervening years. The 1996 running saw three-quarters of the starting field of 43 running at the end. Pole speeds are now in excess of 180 mph on a track that saw the legendary Fireball Roberts earn the track's initial top qualifying honors at just over 130.

The track was designed with a unique double dog-leg front stretch which allows an unusual vantage point for spectators. Its quad oval design has seen as many as 54 lead changes since the 1979 edition of its 600. Although the 600 is the longest race, it has supplied first victories for some drivers. David Pearson (1960), Jeff Gordon (1994), and Bobby Labonte (1995) all recorded their initial career victories on the track which came full cycle from its troubled start to center stage among the event's tracks.

TRACKS

TOO TOUGH TO TAME *As the oldest track on the NASCAR schedule and in many ways the boldest Darlington Raceway is still a daunting prospect for racers.*

Darlington Raceway

It was a bold experiment in 1950. Building a big paved track for stock car racing led some to think Harold Brasington a bit daft. But to do it in a tobacco field in rural South Carolina, as Brasington was, made most people think he'd really gone off the deep end.

Undaunted, he worked on the mile-and-a-quarter, egg-shaped oval, piling up dirt for banked turns when most of the western end had to have a narrower radius, since he hadn't been able to buy the land where the fishing pond lay outside of turn two. The sweeping third and fourth turn at the far end to the east resulted in being more than the normal 180-degrees as a result. And he planned to top the dirt with asphalt (all the tracks at the time had dirt surfaces!) But build it Brasington did.

He aimed for opening the traditional Labor Day weekend of 1950 and met his self-imposed deadline. But when he announced his plan for the race the doubters were more certain than ever that he was crazy.

'A 500-mile race? For stock cars'? Ol' Harold's been out in the sun too long,' was the most common reaction.

With the assistance of big Bill France, they assembled a 75-car field to race for the $25,000 in prize money. Qualifying took two weeks. Curtis Turner was the pole winner at 82.034 mph, but his mark was later topped by Wally Campbell at 82.40. Turner led the three-abreast field to the start but Gober Sosebee shot his Oldsmobile from the outside of the first row to be the event's initial lap leader.

Johnny Mantz, a veteran of AAA competition and the slowest qualifier for the event, employed hard rubber truck tires on the Plymouth he drove for Bill France and flagman Alvin Hawkins, and was the fourth and final race leader of the day. Mantz took the checkered flag with a nine-lap margin some six hours 38 minutes after the starting silk had waved. Fireball Roberts was second, with Red Byron third, despite running 24 tires off the rims of his Cadillac. Observers felt ol' Harold might be smarter than they had thought.

Some 82 cars representing a record 16 makes were on the grid for the second running on Labor Day in 1951, the largest and most diverse field in the division's history. Marshall Teague started 47th and rim-rode the track in his Hudson, taking the lead by the 13th lap in one of the most amazing charges in the sport's history. Although later sidelined by one of the event's many accidents, Teague watched with pleasure as Herb Thomas drove Teague's other Hudson to victory by leading the event's final 294 laps.

Until the 2.5-mile Daytona track opened in 1959, Darlington was the only site of a 500-mile event for NASCAR's major league. It was the circuit's major event, and the track's design makes it one of the most challenging even today, though the bankings have been elevated and the track now measures 1.366 miles in length. It is still the egg-shaped demon which challenged the sport's pioneers with their initial paved surface and inaugural 500 mile race—a track 'Too Tough To Tame.' It is the oldest big track event on the schedule and one of four which are included in The Winston $Million challenge, even though the 1997 Labor Day weekend's 500 saw the track flip-flopped with the front stretch now on what has been the back since 1950.

Harold Brasington had a good idea after all.

Daytona International Speedway

In the mid 1950s, Bill France had a dream of moving his races off the sands of Daytona Beach and onto a big, fast, high-banked track. It took him nearly five years to garner local approval and obtain financing, and construction was accomplished in a cypress swamp near the airport on the undeveloped western side of the city. But it was a magnificent temple of speed when completed and opened in 1959.

Huge 31-degree turns, a 'D' shaped front straight, and 3,000-foot-long back straightaway were unique features of the facility. It was wide and fast, designed for speed and close competition. It proved itself in the inaugural running of the Daytona 500 in 1959.

Cotton Owens was the top qualifier for that first race, with a speed of 143.198 mph when the fastest lap at Darlington hadn't reached the 120mph level. Fifty-nine cars started the race which ran caution-free and resulted in a photo finish between

Lee Petty's Oldsmobile and the Thunderbird piloted by Johnny Beauchamp. No one, even France, expected such a dramatic and close finish. Examining still photos and newsreel footage took three days before Petty was declared the event's winner.

Two winters later, Marvin Panch would drive a year-old Smokey Yunick Pontiac to victory in the prestigious event, doing so at an average speed of 149.601 mph, identical to the third decimal point to the fastest lap turned in Indy 500 qualifying the prior year. Even more recognition fell on France's track and his premier circuit. Not only did they afford close competition but they were fast, too.

Many feel the 1979 Daytona 500 was a turning point for the sport of stock car racing. It was run on a dank, overcast day when most of the eastern US was snow-covered. It was also the first event which CBS TV committed to cover flag-to-flag. Despite a weather-delayed start, the race was close and dramatic. The TV ratings swelled as the event progressed. Snowed-in fans called friends to tell them of this great race they were watching. The friends turned their sets to the race.

The race ended with the two leaders, Cale Yarborough and Donnie Allison, wrecking together for the second time in the event as they headed for the checkered flag on the last lap. Richard Petty swept by the melee and onto his sixth of a record seven victories in the circuit's most important event.

The 1983 edition of the 500 saw an event record 59 lead changes, and the following year Cale Yarborough became the first to break the 200 mph plateau on the track, only to flip his Oldsmobile while trying to enhance it further on his second qualifying lap. His mark was raised to 210.364 mph by Bill Elliott in 1987 trials before speeds were reduced in a concession to safety.

Timing has helped the event's prestige. Since 1982, the 500 has served as the opening event of the Winston Cup season and runs at a time of year when most motorsports in the country are idled by winter's grip. From the track's 24-hour sports car event in late January through the year's biggest motorcycle races in mid-March, the speedway is the focus of racing in America, with the Daytona 500 the crowning jewel of France's dream.

Daytona's Snack-Road Course

When the world land speed record runs moved from the Florida sands in Daytona to the Salt Flats of Utah after Sir Malcolm Campbell's 1935 276.8 mph run, the area was in danger of losing motorsports. The runs had been a mecca for tourism and brought international fame to the area. The city fathers sought something to replace the straight runs up and down the tide-packed sands.

A stock car race, sponsored by the city, appeared to be the answer. Bill France was merely a participant but liked the idea. The event, run north on a unique mile-and-a-half straightaway on the beach and returning south on the two-lane asphalt parallel length of highway A1A, was held with modest success in 1936. Although the promotion lost money, it drew people back to the area and maintained the reputation for racing. Events continued on the course until interrupted by World War II.

Peace brought a resumption of racing on the one-of-a-kind layout with the track refurbished and interest rekindled after five years of hostilities. France, now both driving and promoting the events, watched them grow.

Growing too was home and motel construction in the surrounding area. Coinciding with the 1948 beginning of NASCAR, the track was moved several miles south on the ocean front peninsula and the track lengthened to a 4.2-mile circuit. Two miles up the beach to a tenth-mile

Daytona International Speedway *is the focus of American racing and, as the turning point 1979 Daytona revealed, as it pulled in the many of the nation's snowbound TV viewers, the mild climate is not the least of its advantages. Encompassing the 24 Hour race, the opening race of the Winston Cup season with the 500 and the motorcycle races that occur in mid-March however, weather can't be the only factor in this track's great success.*

limestone turn through the sand dunes it went, then two miles back south on the asphalt road to another tenth mile hairpin turn by the Ponce Inlet lighthouse back onto the sand. It was the design which first carried the cars in competition under the NASCAR banner and held the second event for the 'Strictly Stock' division which would evolve into the Winston Cup Series of today. The circuit was also used for the annual AMA motorcycle racers.

All the NASCAR divisions, Modified, Sportsman, Convertible, and Winston Cup, fought the rutted turns, variable beach conditions and incoming tides over the ensuing 11 seasons. The final auto race on the track ran February 23, 1958, with Paul Goldsmith emerging victorious in a Smokey Yunick-prepared Pontiac. Goldsmith had won on the track in motorcycle racing previously but will be remembered as the last driver to win an auto race on the singular beach road course before the big paved track opened a few miles inland the following winter.

CONTROLLED CHAOS *Daytona's Snack Road course threw many drivers a curve.*

Indianapolis Motor Speedway

Although lacking the stock car history of Darlington and the speeds attained at Daytona or Talladega, the arrival of NASCAR's major league at the renowned 'Brickyard' in 1994 was a spectacular moment in the history of stock car racing. Here were the Fords, Chevrolets, and Pontiacs on the famed surface which had previously entertained the great opened wheel cars of AAA, USAC, and CART. Drivers named Earnhardt, Jarrett, Bodine, and Wallace would race on the heretofore sacred surface where Foyt, Unser, Rose, and Vukovich had battled since the first Indy 500 in 1911.

There had been some testing of the waters before that inaugural 1994 'Brickyard 400' was slated. Two seasons earlier, a handful of NASCAR's top talent had come there from a 'tire test' after a race at Michigan. Thousands were waiting when they arrived and cheered as they took their first tentative laps around the famed two-and-a-half mile rectangular strip of historic asphalt.

The following season, an open test session was held and even more fans were on hand—mostly standing for a better view—as the cars raced, diced, and drafted on the long straights, through the four 90-degree corners and in the short chutes where the high-pitched whine of Offenhausers was replaced by the guttural roar of the unmuffled V-8 engines. It was a show that proved to the few remaining doubters that NASCAR's machines could race on the flat quadrangle.

They came in 1994 to race. The richest event in the sport's history drew the largest crowd ever to witness them compete. They saw Rick Mast, who once traded a cow for his first race car, lead the 43-car field to their double file start by virtue of just the second pole of his career. The drivers thrilled themselves as they raced on the track most had grown up hearing of but doubted they'd ever race on. They thrilled the crowd, too, as 13 of the starters led the race and exchanged the lead 21 times during the 160 laps. Jeff Gordon went on to a half second victory over Brett Bodine and a NASCAR record payday of $613,000 before an estimated 300,000 wildly cheering fans.

The race was a grand success for the track, the fans, the teams, and NASCAR. Once more they had ventured into an uncharted arena to successfully display the brand and quantity of competition which has led the sport to unprecedented heights of success. But in doing so they didn't diminish the allure and magic of the Memorial Day 500, which for more than four score years had dominated American racing with its magnitude, esthetics and, most recently, sheer speed.

The NASCAR teams were back in 1995 and so were the fans. This time they saw Dale Earnhardt's black Chevy beat out Ford-mounted Rusty Wallace by a third of a second to take the richest race payoff of his career. The third time the NASCAR stars ran across the remaining yard of bricks at the track's finish line it was second generation driver Dale Jarrett leading his Yates Racing teammate Ernie Irnan after the 400 miles. Three races and as many different winners.

Some traditionalists were horrified when the 'taxi cabs' of NASCAR announced they would race at Indy. Most have learned the race complements, not competes with, their open-wheeled machines of May, and American motor sports has been the biggest winner.

OVERLEAF: THE BRICKYARD 400 What to some was an abomination and others a distant dream has become a lucrative and welcome addition to American motor sports' racing calendar. Despite the detractors the race has succeeded.

Michigan International Speedway

If there has been a track designed and built for great racing, many fans and competitors feel it is this 'D'-shaped two-mile tri-oval with its 18-degree corner bankings. Wide and smooth, the facility is situated just an hour's drive west of America's automobile capital of Detroit.

The track was built in 1968 by Larry LoPatin's American Raceways, who employed Charles Moneypenny of Daytona Beach to design a perfect track. Moneypenny had been the designer of the Daytona and Talladega tracks (he would later design Richmond's new three-quarter-mile track, also.) Having left his engineering tables in Florida by oversight, Moneypenny utilized materials available at the Detroit library. Those were materials employed in the design of railroads with the required smooth transitions into and out of turns. 'Why not?' he thought, and proceeded with the project. The results proved themselves.

The track had run some sports car and Indy races in 1968 but the big NASCAR boys came in 1969. That season saw the most new tracks come onto the circuit. In addition to the Michigan facility, first time races were held that year at Dover, Delaware, Talladega, Alabama and at a new Texas facility in Bryan, similar to MIS and also owned by LoPatin's group.

The initial NASCAR event here was the 'Motor State 500,' run in mid-June. Donnie Allison was the inaugural pole winner via a 160.135 mph lap, but outside-front-row starter LeeRoy Yarborough took the lead in the initial lap to trigger the first of 35 changes of command during the 250 laps. That created a lead change every seven laps during the race that saw frequent three- and four-wide battles for position and which had a spectacular finish.

Cale Yarborough, driving the Wood brothers' Mercury, and Yarborough, in Junior Johnson's Ford, swapped four times in the final 30 laps. They were still side by side when they got the one-lap to go signal in the front tri-oval. Entering the first turn for the final time, the cars made contact. The white Ford went up the banking and slapped the wall, breaking the steering. Yarborough continued on in the Mercury and slid along the wall before grinding to a stop a hundred yards shy of the finish line. Listed as fourth in the final race rundown, Yarborough climbed from his crumpled machine to a standing ovation from a crowd who'd barely used their seats during the hotly contested event.

Two months later, the NASCAR stars were back for the inaugural 'Yankee 600,' but that one held just 26 lead changes, plus much of the side-by-side battles in the 330 miles run before a steady Michigan rain brought the event to a premature close, with David Pearson driving a Holman-Moody Ford into a soggy victory celebration.

The following year and all the races since have run at a 200-lap, 400-mile distance, but even those have seen as many as 63 lead changes and still feature three, four, and five-wide battles for position in events that have seen the pole speeds top the 185 mph level.

Drafting, speed, and competition have made the Michigan track among the most popular stops on the tour with both the competitors and fans. Its location in the Irish Hills vacation area of the state so synonymous with the auto industry have only added to the significance of the events held on the track that served as a primary pattern for current owner Roger Penske's new California track, which opens in '97.

CROWD PLEASER *The first NASCAR race at MIS got the crowd on their feet. Many haven't sat down since.*

ABSENCE MAKES THE HEART GROW FONDER *After a 21 year break from Watkins Glen NASCAR has had a triumphant return.*

Watkins Glen International

Few oval tracks and no other major road circuit in the country can claim the longevity in NASCAR's big time circuit as the twisting facility in the picturesque Finger Lakes area of upstate New York.

The Watkins Glen course was long noted as the site of the United States Grand Prix where the great cars and drivers of Formula One made their solitary American appearance. Now it is the site of the largest spectator event in the state of New York, a reputation earned by the crowds attracted to the Winston Cup race held here annually since 1986. But the NASCAR association dates back nearly three decades earlier.

In 1957, NASCAR cars first challenged the track. Buck Baker, a former bus driver from Charlotte, North Carolina, would lead a 20-car field into the event in his Chevrolet. The pole winner at 83.064 mph, Baker led the start and every lap as he nosed Fireball Roberts' Ford at the finish.

Historic note: The same day Baker was winning here, Parnelli Jones was winning his first NASCAR event on a road course at Bremerton, Washington. In that era of NASCAR racing, it was not uncommon for two of its major league events to run at the same time on each coast.

The big machines of NASCAR were back at the Glen's track twice in the 1960s, with Billy Wade winning the 1964 visit and Marvin Panch, who'd been Baker's chief challenger a decade earlier, winning in 1965.

Twenty-one years passed before the NASCAR teams came back to Watkins Glen. By then the Formula I event was no longer racing there and the track and that area of the state were economically depressed. Bill France, Jr, having succeeded his father as head of NASCAR and the International Speedway Corporation which owned the Daytona, Talladega and Darlington tracks, was approached to have his major circuit return to boost the track and region. ISC worked out a management agreement with the track, made improvements, and slated the return with brewing giant Anheuser-Busch's Budweiser brand as the major race sponsor.

The result was a huge success. For the opening day of practice a crowd was on hand larger than any event at the track had drawn since the departure of the Grand Prix. Race day was even larger and the hulking stock cars roared around the serpentine asphalt. They raced side by side, changing gears and braking as the fans crowded every vantage point. Tim Richmond drove Rick Hendrick's Chevrolet to victory in the return appearance.

The Glen's races have grown since. Rusty Wallace and Ricky Rudd have triumphed on the demanding track. So have Ernie Irvan and Kyle Petty—the latter's grandfather Lee raced in the '57 event. Mark Martin is a three-time Glen winner and the 1996 edition was won by Geoff Bodine, who grew up in nearby Chemung, New York, and had climbed a tree on the backstretch as a child to get a better view of the 1957 inaugural NASCAR event.

The track and area have rebounded from the depressed economics since this has become a regular stop on the Winston Cup schedule, with the annually-growing crowds drawn here by the competitive battles of NASCAR's stars running atop the faded Grand Prix tire tracks of drivers like Sterling Moss, Jackie Stewart, and Innes Ireland.

STATISTICS

**NASCAR WINSTON CUP CHAMPIONS
(1949 through 1996)**

Car Year	Make No.	Race Driver	Owner	Car	Wins
1949a	22	Red Byron	Raymond Parks	Oldsmobile	2
1950b	60	Bill Rexford	Julian Buesink	Oldsmobile	1
1951	92	Herb Thomas	Herb Thomas	Hudson	7
1952	91	Tim Flock	Ted Chester	Hudson	8
1953	92	Herb Thomas	Herb Thomas	Hudson	11
1954	92		Herb Thomas	Hudson	12
	42	Lee Petty		Chrysler	7
1955	300	Tim Flock	Carl Kiekhaefer	Chrysler	18
1956	300B	Buck Baker	Carl Kiekhaefer	Chrysler	14
1957	87	Buck Baker	Buck Baker	Chevrolet	10
1958	42	Lee Petty	Petty Entrp.	Oldsmobile	7
1959	42	Lee Petty	Petty Entrp.	Plymouth	10
1960	4	Rex White	White-Clements	Chevrolet	6
1961	11	Ned Jarrett	W.G. Holloway, Jr.	Chevrolet	1
1962	8	Joe Weatherly	Bud Moore	Pontiac	9
1963	21		Wood Brothers	Ford	3
	8	Joe Weatherly		Mercury	3
1964	43	Richard Petty	Petty Entrp.	Plymouth	9
1965	11	Ned Jarrett	Bondy Long	Ford	13
1966	6	David Pearson	Cotton Owens	Dodge	14
1967	43	Richard Petty	Petty Entrp.	Plymouth	27
1968	17	David Pearson	Holman-Moody	Ford	16
1969	17	David Pearson	Holman-Moody	Ford	11
1970	71	Bobby Isaac	Nord Krauskopf	Dodge	11
1971	43	Richard Petty	Petty Entrp.	Plymouth	21
1972c	43	Richard Petty	Petty Entrp.	Plymouth	8
1973	72	Benny Parsons	L.G. DeWitt	Chevrolet	1
1974	43	Richard Petty	Petty Entrp.	Dodge	10
1975	43	Richard Petty	Petty Entrp.	Dodge	13
1976	11	Cale Yarborough	Junior Johnson	Chevrolet	9
1977	11	Cale Yarborough	Junior Johnson	Chevrolet	9
1978	11	Cale Yarborough	Junior Johnson	Oldsmobile	10
1979	43	Richard Petty	Petty Entrp.	Chevrolet	5
1980	2	Dale Earnhardt	Rod Osterlund	Chevrolet	5
1981	11	Darrell Waltrip	Junior Johnson	Buick	12
1982	11	Darrell Waltrip	Junior Johnson	Buick	12
1983	22	Bobby Allison	Bill Gardner	Buick	6
1984	44	Terry Labonte	Billy Hagan	Chevrolet	2
1985	11	Darrell Waltrip	Junior Johnson	Chevrolet	3
1986	3	Dale Earnhardt	Richard Childress	Chevrolet	5
1987	3	Dale Earnhardt	Richard Childress	Chevrolet	11

1988	9	Bill Elliott	Harry Melling	Ford	6
1989	27	Rusty Wallace	Raymond Beadle	Pontiac	6
1990	3	Dale Earnhardt	Richard Childress	Chevrolet	9
1991	3	Dale Earnhardt	Richard Childress	Chevrolet	4
1992	7	Alan Kulwicki	Alan Kulwicki	Ford	2
1993	3	Dale Earnhardt	Richard Childress	Chevrolet	6
1994	3	Dale Earnhardt	Richard Childress	Chevrolet	4
1995	24	Jeff Gordon	Rick Hendrick	Chevrolet	7
1996	5	Terry Labonte	Rick Hendrick	Chevrolet	2

a= known as Strictly Stock Division; b= renamed Grand National division; c= renamed Winston Cup Series

ALL-TIME WINSTON CUP RACE WINNERS (1949-1996)

Rank	Driver	Wins
1	Richard Petty	200
2	David Pearson	105
3	Darrell Waltrip	84
	Bobby Allison	84
5	Cale Yarborough	83
6	Dale Earnhardt	70
7	Lee Petty	54
8	Junior Johnson	50
	Ned Jarrett	50
10	Herb Thomas	48
11	Buck Baker	46
	Rusty Wallace	46
13	Bill Elliott	40
	Tim Flock	40
15	Bobby Isaac	37
16	Fireball Roberts	34
17	Rex White	28
18	Fred Lorenzen	26
19	Jim Paschal	25
20	Joe Weatherly	24
21	Benny Parsons	21
	Jack Smith	21
23	Speedy Thompson	20
24	Buddy Baker	19
	Fonty Flock	19
	Davey Allison	19
	Jeff Gordon	19
28	Mark Martin	18
	Harry Gant	18
	Neil Bonnett	18
	Curtis Turner	18
	Geoff Bodine	18
	Terry Labonte	18
34	Marvin Panch	17
	Ricky Rudd	17

In the 1,788 races during the period there have been 148 other drivers who have won at least one event.

BILL ELLIOT *The 1988 Winston Cup Champion.*

RICHARD PETTY *Holder of an incredible 200 Winston Cup race wins.*

TOP 25 WINSTON CUP POLE WINNERS (1949-1996)

Rank	Driver	Poles
1	Richard Petty	127
2	David Pearson	113
3	Cale Yarborough	70
4	Darrell Waltrip	59
5	Bobby Allison	57
6	Bobby Issac	51
7	Bill Elliott	48
8	Junior Johnson	47
9	Buck Baker	46
10	Buddy Baker	40
11	Herb Thomas	38
12	Tim Flock	37
	Fireball Roberts	37
14	Ned Jarrett	36
	Rex White	36
16	Geoff Bodine	35
17	Fred Lorenzen	33
18	Mark Martin	32
19	Fonty Flock	30
20	Marvin Panch	25
	Terry Labonte	25
22	Jack Smith	24
	Alan Kulwicki	24
24	Ricky Rudd	23
25	Dick Hutcherson	22
	Dale Earnhardt	22

DARRELL WALTRIP *Number four of the Top Winston Cup Pole Winners.*

In the 1,747 races where time trials were held (or records kept), there have been 146 other drivers who have won pole positions.

MOST COMPETITIVE RACES

Rank		Event	Lead Track	Race Changes	Race Winner	Laps
1	1984	Winston 500	Talladega, AL	75	Cale Yarborough	188
2	1984	Talladega 500	Talladega, AL	68	Dale Earnhardt	188
3	1978	Talladega 500	Talladega, AL	67	Lennie Pond	188
4	1981	Champion 400	Brooklyn, MI	65	Richard Petty	200
5	1977	Winston 500	Talladega, AL	63	Darrell Waltrip	188
6	1983	Daytona 500	Daytona, FL	59	Cale Yarborough	200
7	1979	Coca Cola 500	Pocono, PA	58	Cale Yarborough	200
8	1979	World 600	Charlotte, NC	54	Darrell Waltrip	400
9	1982	Winston 500	Talladega, AL	51	Darrell Waltrip	188
10	1986	Talladega 500	Talladega, AL	49	Bobby Hillin	188
	1989	DieHard 500	Talladega, AL	49	Terry Labonte	188

Note: In the 1986 Talladega 500 a NASCAR record 26 different drivers, of the 42 who started, officially led the event during the 188 laps.

TOP TEN WINNING WINSTON CUP CAR OWNER WINNERS (ACTIVE)

Rank	Car Owner	Years	Races	Entries	Poles	Wins
1	Petty Enterprises	48	1,649	2,009	148	269
2	Junior Johnson*	31	839	1,071	128	139
3	Wood Brothers	44	875	898	116	96
4	Richard Childress	23	643	651	24	63
	Bud Moore	33	922	958	43	63
6	Rick Hendrick	13	384	968	74	60
7	Harry Melling	15	390	390	40	34
8	Robert Yates	8	237	271	17	27
9	Jack Roush	9	268	450	36	18
10	Morgan-McClure	14	353	353	12	13

* Retired at end of 1996 season.

BOBBY HILLIN *Winner of the testing 1986 Talladega 500.*

WINS BY CAR MAKE*
(1949-1996)

Ford	445
Chevrolet	434
Plymouth	190
Dodge	162
Pontiac	119
Oldsmobile	116
Mercury	96
Hudson	79
Buick	65
Chrysler	59
Thunderbird*	6
AMC Matador	5
Lincoln	4
Studebaker	3
Nash	1
Jaguar	1

* Thunderbird listed as separate make in 1959. Now included under Ford. Three other races won by Grand American Division cars (i.e. Chevrolet Camaro, Ford Mustang) in combined events not shown in the above totals for 1,788 races.

RACE RECORDS AT CURRENT WINSTON CUP TRACKS

Atlanta Motor Speedway (1.522 mile)
500 miles: 163.633 mph by Dale Earnhardt, Chev., Nov. 8, 1996

Bristol Motor Speedway (0.533 mile)
500 Laps: 101.074 mph by Charlie Glotzbach, Chev., July 11, 1971

Charlotte Motor Speedway (1.5 mile)
600 miles: 151.952 mph by Bobby Labonte, Chev., May 28, 1995.
500 miles: 154.537 mph by Ernie Irvan, Ford, Oct. 10, 1993

Darlington Raceway (1.366 mile)
500 miles: 137.958 mph by Dale Earnhardt, Chev., March 28, 1993
400 miles: 132.703 mph by David Pearson, Ford, May 11, 1968

Daytona International Speedway (2.5 miles)
500 miles: 177.602 mph by Buddy Baker, Oldsmobile, Feb. 17, 1980
400 miles: 173.473 mph by Bobby Allison, Mercury, July 4, 1980

Dover Downs Speedway (1.0 mile)
500 miles: 125.945 mph by Bill Elliott, Ford, Sept. 16, 1990

Indianapolis Motor Speedway (2.5 mile)
400 miles: 155.206 mph by Jeff Gordon, Aug. 5, 1995

Martinsville Speedway (0.526 mile)
500 laps: 82.223 mph by Jeff Gordon, Chev., Sept. 22, 1996

Michigan Speedway (2.0 mile)
400 miles: 166.033 mph by Rusty Wallace, Ford, June 21, 1996

New Hampshire Speedway (1.058 mile)
300 laps: 107.029 mph by Jeff Gordon, Chev., July 9, 1995

North Carolina Motor Speedway (1.017 mile)
400 miles: 122.320 mph by Ricky Rudd, Ford, Oct. 26, 1996

Phoenix International Raceway (1.0 mile)
312 miles: 109.709 mph by Bobby Hamilton, Pontiac, Oct. 27, 1996

Pocono International Raceway (2.5 mile)
500 miles: 144.892 mph by Rusty Wallace, Ford, July 21, 1996

Richmond International Raceway (0.75 mile)
300 miles: 108.499 mph by Rusty Wallace, Ford, March 2, 1997

Sears Point Raceway (2.52 mile Road Course)
187 miles: 81.413 mph by Ernie Irvan, Chevrolet, June 7, 1992

Talladega Superspeedway (2.66 mile)
500 miles: 188.354*mph by Mark Martin, Ford, May 10, 1997
* Fastest point race in NASCAR history
(second fastest 500 mile race in American Motor Sports).

Texas Motor speedway (1.5 mile) [opened April 1997]
500 miles: 125.111 mph by Jeff Burton, Ford, April 6, 1997

Watkins Glen (2.45 mile Road Course)
220.5 miles: 103.030 mph by Mark Martin, Ford, Aug. 9, 1996

RICHARD PETTY AND BOBBY HAMILTON *Another successful season in 1996.*

63

INDY CAR

Indy car racing has always been the ultimate form of single seat, open wheel racing in North America. Since the early 1900s, young drivers serving their racing apprenticeship on the quarter-and-half mile tracks that dot the American landscape have dreamed of racing Indy cars. While an increasing number of short track drivers have gone on to success in stock car racing, their place has been taken by a new breed of Indy drivers who cut their teeth on road courses in America and around the world.

One of the central features of Indy car racing in the 1990s is that the sport is no longer strictly an American phenomenon. Although Americans like Michael Andretti, Al Unser, Jr. and Jimmy Vasser have continued to bring home race wins and championships, they are competing with a veritable United Nations of drivers ranging from Formula One veterans to up and coming stars from all corners of the globe.

Just as the men who compete in Indy car racing form a melting pot of driving talent, so the heritage of the cars they race is highly multi-national, with chassis made in America and Europe powered by engines with roots in Detroit and Stuttgart, England and Japan. Today's PPG CART World Series also features a number of events on foreign soil with events in Canada, Australia, Brazil and Japan, with the possibility of

RACING

Europe entering not too far down the road.

However, one of the salient features of Indy car racing has always been that the organizations in charge of the sport have tried to keep the impact of new technologies in check to ensure that the human element (aka the drivers) remains paramount. A half century ago rulesmakers concerned with rising costs and escalating speeds introduced regulations to enable low cost, production-based vehicles to compete against pure-bred racing machines. The 1960s saw the breathtaking turbine cars regulated to the point they became uncompetitive, while the 80s and '90s have witnessed ongoing battles to limit the effectiveness of aerodynamic devices and a host of electronic aids born of the computer age.

The conflicting interests in the sport have not always seen eye to eye on the issues of the day. From the drivers' strike at the 1948 Indy 500 to the breakaway of Championship Auto Racing Teams from the United States Auto Club in 1979, Indy car racing has seen its share of controversy. That turbulent history continues today with CART sanctioning its PPG CART World Series even as the new Indy Racing League pursues its own path geared towards oval tracks, American drivers and strict controls on the prices and availability of equipment.

While most observers agree this regular internecine strife has handicapped efforts to bring Indy car racing to the very forefront of the American sporting scene, the legacy of political turmoil reflects the fierce passions the sport engenders in participants, constituents and fans alike.

Frustrating and maddening, to be sure, Indy car politics is seldom dull.

THE HISTORY

TOMMY MILTON *Here winning the 1923 Indy 500, thus becoming the first person to win it twice.*

RAY HARROUN *Won the inaugural Indy 500 in the Marmon Wasp in 1911, two years after Indianapolis Motor Speedway opened.*

One of America's most prestigious forms of motor racing for nearly a century, Indy car racing has attracted a major international following in recent years. With a worldwide television audience topping one billion and crowds in excess of 100,000 at each event, the PPG CART World Series offers Indy car racing fans the excitement of wheel-to-wheel racing at 240 mph, and its competitors the varied challenges of permanent road courses, mile ovals, super-speedways and temporary street circuits. Meanwhile, the rival Indy Racing League boasts the world's largest single day sporting event—the Indianapolis 500—and a slate of oval track races designed to attract competitors from America's 'grass roots' tracks to Indy car racing.

Many legends of Indy car racing also enjoyed success on the world stage; men like World Champions Mario Andretti, Emerson Fittipaldi and Nigel Mansell, as well as Jimmy Murphy, winner of the 1921 French Grand Prix and Dan Gurney, a four time winner in Formula One who teamed with Indy car legend A.J. Foyt to win

the 24 Hours of Le Mans in 1967. Others, like Foyt, Al Unser, Rodger Ward, Rex Mays and Tommy Milton, etched their names in American folklore based largely on their success in Indy cars.

These drivers are part and parcel of the longest-running, continuously contested motor racing championship in the world. Although Indy car racing's ultimate origins are the subject of debate among historians, the forerunners of today's Indy car series date to the turn of the century when the American Automobile Association (AAA) began sanctioning races on open roads. The country's first ever purpose-built racing track—the Indianapolis Motor Speedway—opened in 1909 and two years later Ray Harroun's Marmon Wasp won the inaugural Indy 500.

By 1916 the AAA had established a series of 13 races at a variety of venues around the country, including high-banked, wooden 'board' tracks, road races and the Indianapolis 'Brickyard' (named for the millions of bricks

used to pave the track in 1910), widely viewed as the first national championship; a championship won by an Englishman—Dario Resta—driving a French-built Peugeot.

The AAA championship gained momentum during the Roaring Twenties, with as many as 26 events—primarily on board tracks—counting towards the national championship in a single season. At a time when much of the country still relied on oat-fed, four-legged, single-horsepower transportation, men like Milton, Murphy, and Frank Lockhart raced wheel-to-wheel at upwards of 150 mph. Two dozen events in the 1926 championship were won at average speeds in excess of 100 mph with Lockhart setting a record at Charlotte that stood for more than thirty years.

The Golden Age of Indy car racing came to an end with the Great Depression. The costly board tracks fell into disrepair and the AAA instituted new rules designed to reduce speeds and limit the skyrocketing costs of equipment. As the economy

collapsed, so the AAA championship dwindled to four, three and finally two races per season. Nevertheless, the era produced noteworthy drivers such as Louis Meyer and Wilbur Shaw, the first three time winners of the Indianapolis 500, and saw European greats Tazio Nuvolari and Bernd Rosemeyer win races at the elaborate Roosevelt Park Raceway road circuit on Long Island.

With the onset of World War II, Indy car racing went into a hibernation that left the Indianapolis Motor Speedway in ruin after five years of neglect. Resurrected by local businessman Tony Hulman and World War I hero Eddie Rickenbacker (a seven time winner on the AAA circuit), Indianapolis became the hub of a revitalized national championship contested largely on mile long dirt ovals across the country. This era was dominated by colorful characters like Tony Bettenhausen, Bill 'The Mad Russian' Vukovich and cigar-chomping Jimmy Bryan.

The AAA bowed-out of racing after the horrific accident at the 24 Hours of Le Mans in 1955, and a new organization—the United States Auto Club—took control of a national championship that evolved into a balanced mixture of paved and dirt ovals.

The 1960s and '70s produced some of America's greatest racing heroes in Foyt, Andretti and the brothers Unser: Al and Bobby. More recently, drivers trained on the road circuits of North America have found a home in Indy car racing; men such as Bobby Rahal and Michael Andretti, even as Rick Mears emerged from off-road racing and Al Unser, Jr. apprenticed in everything from sprint cars to Can-Am monsters.

In 1979 a new organization headed by the team owners—Championship Auto Racing Teams—assumed control of the Indy car series. Under the auspices of CART, new events were added at road courses and at several temporary street circuits in major metropolitan areas, and national television coverage grew by leaps and bounds. Indy car racing's new high profile spurred a massive increase in commercial sponsorship of the sport, headed by PPG Industries, sponsor of the CART series. Those trends continued in the 1990s, along with unparalleled international recognition thanks to the success of one time Formula One stars like Fittipaldi and Mansell in the PPG CART World Series.

No less storied than the heroes of Indy car racing is the fascinating cavalcade of machinery that has competed in the sport over the years. From the days when modified production cars struggled to average 100 mph at Indianapolis, to the magical era of hand-built Duesenbergs and Millers in the 1920s, the championship has been a battleground for some of the greatest names in the automotive industry. Even in the midst of the Great Depression, Ford and Hudson continued to contest the championship and, later, Wilbur Shaw won two straight Indy 500s in a Maserati.

The 1950s were dominated by the famed Offenhauser engine, which powered all but one of the decade's race winners in front-engined roadsters and sprint cars despite annual, loud and powerful challenges from the Novi at Indianapolis. In the 1960s the Granatelli family, who were so instrumental in the Novi cars, introduced two of the most controversial cars in racing history to the sport: the STP turbines. Powered by Pratt & Whitney turbines, the cars whistled around the Indianapolis Motor Speedway for two years before they were effectively outlawed by a series of rule changes.

While the turbines were banned, the other major development of the 1960s—rear-engined cars—quickly gained ascendancy, opening the door to a powerful European influence in the sport that continues to this day.

England, for example, was home to the Chevrolet-financed Ilmor V8 (winning 65 of 68 races from 1988 through early 1992), while Indy car racing's growing international popularity attracted other major automotive players in the 1980s, including Porsche and Alfa Romeo. After a 20 year absence, Ford returned to Indy car racing in partnership with Cosworth Engineering in 1992, to be joined in 1994 by Mercedes-Benz and Honda, with Toyota entering the fray in 1996.

Likewise, English chassis makers March, Lola and Reynard have dominated Indy car racing in

THE FORCE *Bill Vukovich (pictured here in 1951) was a force to be reckoned with until his tragic death in the 1954 Indy 500.*

KEEP IT IN THE FAMILY *Al Unser, Jr. has a difficult task trying to keep ahead of his father and uncle who are both Indy legends.*

recent years, as teams turned away from building their own cars in favor of mass-produced 'customer' cars. Even Penske Racing, which produces its own chassis, bases its manufacturing operations in England. 1996, however, saw a revival of the American chassis, first in All American Racers' Eagle, and later with the news that Swift Engineering would produce chassis for Newman/Haas Racing in 1997.

In response to the foreign influence in Indy car racing and the climbing costs accompanying the greatly increased commercial involvement in the sport, Indianapolis Motor Speedway president Tony George established a separate Indy car series in 1996 called the Indy Racing League. By running exclusively on oval tracks and instituting strict price controls on engines and chassis, the IRL hoped to create new opportunities for American drivers and to lower the costs associated with Indy car racing.

The divisions between CART and the IRL gave rise to a contentious season of racing in 1996, one sullied by various legal suits and climaxed by CART holding its own 'US 500' at Michigan Speedway in direct competition with the Indianapolis 500. Despite the loss of the one time centerpiece of its series, CART enjoyed a successful season in 1996. The IRL attracted disappointing crowds for most of its events, but race day turnout at the Indianapolis 500 was the usual 350,000 strong.

The subsequent settlement of legal action, in which neither the IRL nor CART claimed victory, coupled with CART's decision not to schedule a race in competition with the 1997 Indy 500, created a welcome, if uneasy, truce between the two groups. And while CART appears capable of continuing its policy of controlled domestic and international growth—adding a race in Japan in 1998 for example—it remains to be seen whether the IRL will be able to attract the fans and sponsors needed to sustain its series outside the boundaries of the Indianapolis Motor Speedway.

ANDRETTI

THE GREAT

Mario Andretti: arguably history's most versatile racing driver.

He repeated as Indy car champion twice in the next four years and rebounded from a firey crash in practice to score what was destined to be his only Indianapolis 500 victory in 1969. The previous year he won the pole position in his Formula One debut at the US Grand Prix, and the 1970s saw him take an increasingly active role in Formula One and sports car racing. Although he scored his first Grand Prix win for Ferrari, his Formula One career reached its climax with Lotus. After four wins in 1977, he dominated the 1978 season, winning six times and claiming the World Driving Championship.

Andretti returned to Indy cars full time in 1983 with a team owned by veteran Carl Haas and movie star Paul Newman. He won six races in 1984 en route to his fourth Indy car title and added ten more wins in the next nine seasons. After four productive years with his son Michael as his teammate, Andretti was joined at Newman/Haas by Nigel Mansell in 1993. Ironically, his final win came at Phoenix International Raceway that year, a day after his celebrated new teammate had been hospitalized in the wake of a crash in practice.

Andretti won the 1978 World Driving Championship, the 1967 Daytona 500 and a host of international sports car events, including the 1967, 1970 and 1972 12 Hours of Sebring. His greatest success, however, came in Indy cars. He is a four time champion and ranks first in career poles (66) and second in wins (52) despite spending some of his most productive years racing in Europe.

Andretti emigrated from Italy to the eastern Pennsylvania hamlet of Nazareth with his family in 1955 and, unbeknownst to his parents, was soon racing at local tracks along with his brother Aldo. While injuries would force Aldo out of racing, Mario raced modifieds, midgets and sprint cars before making his first Indy car start in mid-1964. The following season, Andretti scored his first Indy car win at Indianapolis Raceway Park on the way to the first of his four national championships.

DRIVERS

Ralph DePalma was not only the first truly great American racing driver, he remains one of the great heroes of American sports history thanks to his legendary sense of fair play.

Though he won hundreds of races throughout his career, perhaps DePalma's most famous race was one he did not win—the 1912 Indianapolis 500. There DePalma and riding mechanic Rupert Jeffkins pushed their Mercedes to the finish line when it broke a connecting rod after leading the first 197 laps of the race; DePalma was among the first to congratulate winner Joe Dawson.

Born in Italy in 1883, DePalma and his family emigrated to the United States in 1889. He began racing in his mid-teens and utterly dominated dirt track racing in the United States before joining the national championship chase in 1912. That year he won the first of his two national titles with four wins on the Santa Monica and Elgin, Illinois road courses. He repeated that success at Santa Monica and Elgin in 1914 on the way to his second championship and the following year took his only Indy 500 win in a Mercedes 'Grey Ghost' that lost a cylinder in the closing laps.

DePalma went on to continued success in the AAA championship, driving for Packard and Ballot. In 1920 he carved another niche for himself in the Indianapolis 500 annals when, after his Ballot caught fire with a two lap lead over Gaston Chevrolet, DePalma crawled out on the hood with a fire extinguisher in a vain effort to douse the flames.

Although DePalma continued to race the AAA championship and at Indianapolis well into the 1920s, he later went back to his dirt track roots and won the Canadian championship in 1926.

71

FOYT

Indy car racing's all time leader in wins (67), 'Super Tex' is a seven time champion and was the first driver to win the Indianapolis 500 four times.

An outstanding midget and sprint car driver, Foyt was also successful in stock car and sports car racing, winning several USAC stock car titles and the Daytona 500 as well as the 24 Hours of Le Mans and the 24 Hours of Daytona. He is the only driver in history to win the Indianapolis 500, the Daytona 500 and the 24 Hours of Le Mans.

Learning his craft as the son of a respected mechanic, Foyt worked as a racing mechanic during his early teens before building and racing his own stock car on local tracks. He graduated to midgets and sprint cars, and made his first start at Indianapolis in 1958. Two years later he won his first Indy car championship and, in 1961, captured his first Indianapolis 500.

Foyt went on to win four more titles and two Indy 500s by 1967, setting records that still stand for wins in a season (ten) and consecutive victories (seven) in 1964.

Foyt's success was not limited to Indy cars, however. He teamed with Dan Gurney to win the 1967 24 Hours of Le Mans and also won the 1968 USAC stock car championship, the 1971 USAC Dirt Car championship and the 1972 Daytona 500.

After running limited Indy car schedules in the early 1970s, Foyt won his sixth national championship in 1975 and a record-setting fourth Indy 500 in 1977. He took his second straight International Race of Champions title that same year and, after

adding a second USAC stock car crown to his accomplishments in 1978, earned his final USAC Indy car championship in 1979. Although he would win just one more Indy car race (in 1981), Foyt continued to enjoy success in sports car racing, winning the 24 Hours of Daytona (1983 and '85) and the 1985 12 Hours of Sebring.

After suffering serious injuries in an accident at the 1990 Road America Indy car race, at age 56 he made a miraculous comeback by qualifying second fastest for the 1991 Indianapolis 500. In an emotionally charged moment at Indianapolis in 1993, Foyt announced his retirement from Indy car racing although he has since competed in stock cars on occasion.

A three time Indy car champion, Al Unser trails only A.J. Foyt and Mario Andretti in career wins (39) and laps led (5812).

One of three drivers to win championship races on a paved oval, a dirt track and a road course in one year, Unser is also one of three drivers with four Indianapolis 500 wins and is the all time leader in laps led at Indianapolis (644).

The youngest of the second generation of racing Unsers, Al began racing a modified stock car built by his father and brother Bobby at age 17. He raced progressively faster modifieds and sprint cars throughout the Southwest, earning his first major success at Pike's Peak in 1964.

He made his Indy car debut that same year and, after several seasons of modest success, scored five consecutive wins in 1968 and five more victories the following season. Then, in one of Indy car racing's greatest seasons, Unser won ten races—including the Indianapolis 500—to take the 1970 Indy car title. He became the fourth driver to win back-to-back Indy 500s with a second win in 1971 and in 1978 became the only driver in history to win Indy car's Triple Crown of 500 mile events, winning his third Indy 500 as well as the Pocono and California 500s.

Also known for his versatility, Unser won the 1973 USAC dirt car crown and a Formula 5000 race at Road America in 1975 and two straight IROC championships (1977 and '78).

Unser joined Penske Racing in 1983 and promptly won his second Indy car championship but was slated for a back-up role in 1985 while teammate Rick Mears recovered from injuries suffered the previous season. But Mears stepped aside when Unser emerged as a championship contender, and Al ultimately edged his son Al, Jr., by one point to take his third Indy car title. Two years later, he qualified a one-year-old March 86C for the 1987 Indianapolis 500 and went on to become the race's second four time winner. Unser continued to pinch-hit for Penske and other teams over the next several years before announcing his retirement in 1994.

WARD

Rodger Ward overcame a checkered start to his Indy car career to become a two time national champion and two time Indy 500 winner. He ranks eighth on the list of all time Indy car race winners.

A fighter pilot in World War II, Ward began racing in 1946 while stationed in Wichita Falls, Texas, before returning to his native California where he continued his career driving midgets and stock cars. After a couple of years on the national midget circuit, Ward made his first Indianapolis start in 1951 but dropped out after 34 laps with a broken oil line.

Ward earned his first championship victories in 1953 with back to back wins at Springfield and Detroit, but was involved in a couple of fatal accidents in 1954 and '55—including the one that took the life of the great Bill Vukovich during the Indy 500—which nearly caused him to retire.

Known as a hard-drinking womanizer, Ward turned over a new leaf in the aftermath of the Vukovich accident. He gave up drinking, married and gradually worked his way to the top echelon of Indy car drivers. He earned his first wins in five years in 1957 and two more in 1958, before joining Bob Wilke's Leader Card team to drive A.J. Watson's upright roadster in 1959.

The combination quickly proved effective, with Ward coming home second at Trenton in April before leading 130 laps on the way to his first Indy 500 win. He went on to four more wins and his first national title in 1959 and either finished first (1961), second (1960, '63 and '64) or third (1962) in the next five seasons. He earned his second Indy 500 victory in 1962, won five of 12 events in 1962 and raced actively until the 1966 season when he earned his 26th and final Indy car win at Phoenix.

TOP INDY RACERS

Michael Andretti

After operating in the shadow of his illustrious father for several years, Andretti became a force in his own right in the late 1980s. After three runner-up finishes in the PPG Cup race (1986, '87 and '90), he scored eight wins and led more than 45% of the racing laps in 1991 to take his first Indy car title. Despite leading more than 50% of the laps, he was forced to settle for another second place finish in the 1992 PPG points race. Following a fruitless sortee in Formula One with Team McLaren, Andretti returned to Indy cars in 1994 and has since taken the lead in career victories among active drivers with 35 heading into 1997.

Tony Bettenhausen

Racer Melvin Eugene 'Tony' Bettenhausen won just about everything there was to win in Indy car racing: 21 races; the 1951 and '58 national titles. He won more poles and led more miles and more laps than any other driver in the 1950s. But the one prize that eluded him was the Indianapolis 500. He finished second in 1955, fourth in 1958 and 1959, but never had the good fortune and good machinery needed to win the Memorial Day Classic. Bettenhausen had perhaps his best chance to win at Indy in 1961, when he set the pace in practice and was favored to win the pole position. But he lost his life the day before qualifying when he crashed while testing the car of his friend Paul Russo. Bettenhausen's sons Tony, Gary and Merle continued the family's racing legacy, with Gary a four time Indy car winner, and Tony, a former Indy car driver himself, now running the Bettenhausen Racing team.

Jimmy Bryan

Jimmy 'The Arizona Cowboy' Bryan epitomized the brash, hell-bent-for-leather style of many Indy car drivers in the 1950s. After cutting his teeth on the dirt tracks of the Southwest and the West Coast, he made his first Indy car start in 1952 and, in 1954, won the final four races of the year to earn the first of his three national titles. Though he won six of 11 races the following season he finished second in the title chase, but Bryan rebounded to win back-to-back titles in 1956 and '57. 1957 also saw him win the Race of Two Worlds Trophy which pitted the stars and cars of Indy car racing against some of Europe's top drivers on the high banked track at Monza, Italy. The following year Bryan led 139 of 200 laps to win the Indy 500 but in 1960 he died in a crash at Pennsylvania's Langhorne Speedway.

Earl Cooper

One of the world's first truly great drivers, 'The Earl of Cooper' was a force in American racing from its infancy up through the Roaring Twenties, with three national championships and 20 Indy car wins to his name. Cooper's greatest success came through his association with Harry Stutz' cars, with which he won his three titles in 1913, '15 and '17 and then promptly went into

MICHAEL ANDRETTI
The future looks bright for this racer.

semi-retirement. He began racing full time again in 1921, winning races in both Duesenbergs and Millers and taking second in the 1924 national championship. The one prize that proved elusive, however, was the Indianapolis 500. Cooper spun out while leading in 1913, suffered a blown tire while contending for the 1923 victory, set fastest lap in 1925 but crashed and won the pole in 1926 only to go out early with transmission problems. He retired in 1928 after an uncompetitive showing at Indianapolis.

Emerson Fittipaldi

The two time World Champion (1972 and '74) enjoyed a successful second career in Indy cars, and his presence spurred the growth of the sport's popularity in South America in the 1990s. Fittipaldi came out of retirement to drive for some marginal Indy

car teams in 1983, then joined Patrick Racing and scored the first of his 21 career victories in 1985. He went on to win the 1989 PPG Cup and Indy 500 with Patrick before joining Penske Racing and earning ten more wins, including a second Indy 500 in 1993, before suffering what are likely to be career-ending injuries in a crash in the 1996 Michigan 500.

Dan Gurney

Gurney achieved cult-hero status for his exploits in Formula One, including the 1967 Belgian Grand Prix where he became the first (and only) American to win a Grand Prix in a car of his own design: the All American Racers' Eagle. Also a winner in Can-Am, Trans-Am, sports cars, endurance racing, stock cars and sedans, Gurney won seven Indy car races and twice finished second at Indianapolis, despite never

devoting his full attention to that arena of the sport. His greatest impact on Indy cars came after he retired as a driver, when his Eagle chassis rewrote the record books in the early 1970s. After a ten year hiatus from the sport, Gurney and AAR returned to Indy car racing in 1996.

Gordon Johncock

Fast and fearless, 'Gordy' was virtually synonymous with Patrick Racing through the 1970s and '80s, an era which saw the former supermodified driver earn 18 of his 25 Indy car victories. Sadly, Johncock's first big win came in a race that everyone else wanted to forget—the 1973 Indianapolis 500—an event in which three drivers and a crewman lost their lives. Fortunately, Johncock's second Indianapolis victory came under altogether better circumstances as he withstood a furious

charge by Rick Mears to win by a scant .16 seconds; which was, at that time, the closest Indy 500 in history.

Parnelli Jones

Rufus Parnelli Jones rose from humble beginnings as the son of an Oklahoma farmer to become one of the most gifted racing drivers of his generation. He cut his racing teeth on the dirt tracks of Southern California, led the 1961 Indy 500 as a rookie and won the race in 1963 despite the fact that his car was leaking oil at an alarming rate. One of only two drivers to beat Foyt in 1964, Jones nearly earned a second Indy 500 win in 1967 driving the controversial STP Turbine which dominated the race until a mechanical failure just three laps from finish. Despite racing Indy cars for just a few seasons, Jones ranks 16th on the all time list of pole winners, with 12.

DAN GURNEY *Racer and designer Gurney's impact on Indy was arguably greatest after his retirement when, in the 1970s, his chassis rewrote the record books.*

Nigel Mansell

Named the 'The Lion' by Italian Formula One race fanatics, the 'Tifosi', Mansell competed in just 31 Indy car races, but his impact on the sport can hardly be overstated. Mansell joined Newman/Haas Racing in 1993 as the reigning World Champion in the wake of an extended contract wrangle with the Williams Formula One team. He brought his massive following along with him, thus introducing a world-wide audience to Indy car racing. Mansell stormed to five wins, seven poles and the 1993 PPG Cup. Despite being a total novice to oval track racing at the beginning of the season, he won on the ovals at Milwaukee, Michigan and, after an epic three way battle with Emerson Fittipaldi and Paul Tracy, at New Hampshire. Although he returned to Formula One after the 1994 season, racing fans around the world continued watching the PPG CART World Series in record numbers.

Rex Mays

The bare statistics—eight wins in fifteen seasons—only hint at the impact the hard charging Mays had on Indy car racing in the 1930s and '40s. More impressive is the fact that he won no less than 19 pole positions out of 34 races between 1936 and '46 in an era of curtailed schedules owing to the Depression, and later, World War II. Mays was crowned national champion twice (1940 and '41) on the strength of two wins in the season's three races, although ironically, he never won the race that counted most in the public's eye—the Indianapolis 500—before his fatal crash at the Del Mar fairgrounds near San Diego in 1949.

LEFT: PARNELLI JONES *A farm boy turned racing hero.*
BELOW: NIGEL MANSELL *'The Lion' who roared onto the Indy racing scene.*

Joe Leonard

'Pelican' Joe enjoyed a brief but successful Indy car career. The former American Motorcycle Association champion made his Indy car debut in 1964, earning his first win at Milwaukee in 1970. The following season he won the California 500 on the way to his first Indy car title and in 1972, as part of the Vels Parnelli 'Super Team,' out-distanced teammates Al Unser and Mario Andretti to win a second straight Indy car championship on the strength of consecutive wins at Michigan, Pocono and Milwaukee. Sadly, Leonard suffered ankle injuries at Ontario in 1974 and never regained his championship form.

Frank Lockhart

Considered by many to be among the most talented drivers in Indy car history, Lockhart had a brilliant but tragically short career. After dominating America's dirt tracks as a teenager, Lockhart made his first Indy car start in 1925 and the following season earned his first win as a rookie in a rain-shortened Indianapolis 500. That win was followed by nine victories on the country's fearsome board tracks over the next year and a half, good enough to finish runner-up in the 1926 and '27 national titles. Lockhart died the following year in a crash at Daytona Beach during an attempt to establish a new land speed record.

Rick Mears

Respected by his fellow competitors, adored by the public, and held in the highest esteem by the media, Mears was the most accomplished Indy car oval track racer of his era and the only driver in CART history to win all the road course events in a single season (1981). A three time PPG Cup champion (1979, '81 and '82) with Penske Racing, Mears joined A.J. Foyt and Al Unser in 1991 as a four time winner of the Indianapolis 500. He stands alone, however, as the only man to win the pole position at Indianapolis six times. Despite missing parts of two seasons after a serious accident in 1984, Mears ranks third on CART's all time list of winners (26).

Louis Meyer

A three time national champion (1928, '29 and '33), Meyer became the first driver to win three Indianapolis 500s with victories in 1928, 1933 and 1936. A versatile driver, Meyer won on the boards at Altoona, the dirt at Detroit and, of course, the bricks at Indianapolis. His early success came in supercharged, front wheel drive Miller 91s, while his later victories came in the 'Junk Formula,' and his final Indy 500 win came in a year when AAA officials imposed dramatic restrictions in fuel economy. But Meyer's impact on Indy car goes beyond his accomplishments behind the wheel. A top notch mechanic and businessman, he joined with Dale Drake to buy Fred Offenhauser's engine business in 1946 and subsequently refined and improved the basic four cylinder engine to the point that it remained a potent force in Indy car racing well into the '70s.

RICK MEARS *A man of many records.*

Tommy Milton

Born of a wealthy family and blind in one eye, Tommy Milton was an unlikely candidate to become one of the early greats of Indy racing. He began racing the Midwest circuit in 1913 and moved up to the AAA series in 1916 with the Duesenberg team. The following year he scored his first major success on the concrete oval at Providence, Rhode Island, and went on to 'win' the disputed national championship in 1920 (records on how many races comprised the AAA's official championship are inconclusive, although many historians believe the title was won by Gaston Chevrolet). Milton was the undisputed winner of the 1921 championship, with four wins, a second and three thirds. The following year he scored the first of his two Indy 500 victories, finishing two laps clear of second placed Roscoe Sarles, and in 1923 became the first two time winner of the event.

Ralph Mulford

A two time national champion and winner of 17 Indy car races, Mulford may be best known for his role in the inaugural Indianapolis 500 where he was credited with second place behind Ray Harroun. Mulford (and others) contended officials failed to score a lap he completed owing to the confusion surrounding a crash that wiped out the timers' stand. Although he would never win the Indy 500, Mulford won plenty of other races, including the 1911 Vanderbilt Cup race in Savannah in which he outlasted the great Ralph DePalma to take a victory that helped secure the first of his two AAA titles. Mulford's early success came with the Lozier cars, but after 1911 he drove a variety of cars including Duesenbergs, Mercedes,

Peugeots and Frontenac, earning three wins on the Uniontown board track in the latter to edge DePalma for the 1918 national title.

Jimmy Murphy

One of Indy car racing's first stars, Murphy earned nineteen wins in just five seasons in the early 1920s. Protege of two time national champion Tommy Milton, Murphy made his first start in the final race of 1919 and earned his first win in the 1920 season opener at Beverly Hills. The following year he became the last driver to win a Grand Prix race in an American-built car—a Duesenberg—for more than fifty years when he captured the French Grand Prix. He earned the first of his two national championships and his only Indy 500 win in 1922 and, after finishing runner-up in the 1923 championship, was crowned posthumous champion in 1924 after a fatal crash at Syracuse.

Bobby Rahal

The only three time PPG Cup winner (1986, '87 and '92), Rahal came to Indy car racing via Formula Atlantic, sports cars, the Can-Am and Formula One. After earning two wins in his first season of Indy car racing (1982), he recorded an emotional victory in the 1986 Indianapolis 500, days before team owner Jim Trueman succumbed to cancer. Rahal went on to win the PPG Cup that season, repeating as Indy car champion in 1987. He formed his own team with Carl Hogan in 1992 and promptly won his third PPG Cup. After Rahal/Hogan's efforts to build its own chassis and establish a partnership with Honda came to naught, Rahal struck out on his own to form Team Rahal, in

BOBBY RAHAL *The only three time PPG cup winner can afford to smile.*

search of a 25th Indy car win and a fourth PPG Cup.

Johnny Rutherford

The original 'JR' from Texas, Rutherford's gentlemanly off-track demeanor stood in marked contrast to his firey style behind the wheel. A graduate of the Southwest modified racing scene, Rutherford made his first Indy car start in 1962 and earned the first of his 27 career wins in 1965. Nine years and two serious accidents elapsed before his second Indy car win, but the 1970s saw him win twenty times. He joined Team McLaren in 1973 and promptly won his first Indianapolis pole, then won two of the next three Indy 500s in 1974 and 1976. In 1980 Rutherford teamed with fellow Texan Jim Hall to win a third Indianapolis 500 in the Chaparral 2K on the way to the PPG Championship.

JOHNNY RUTHERFORD *His doggedly determined racing style stood at odds with his off-track racing gallantry. He had a nine year wait in between Indy victories in a career that stretched from the '60s to the '80s.*

Mauri Rose

Mauri Rose became the third man to win three Indy 500s with consecutive victories in 1947 and 1948 to go along with his win in 1941 in relief of Floyd Davis. Rose' career might have included more wins but for the fact that it was interrupted for four years by World War II. Rose first raced Indy cars during the depths of the Depression in the days of the 'Junk Formula' and riding mechanics. His first win

came at Detroit in 1932 and he won his first Indy 500 nine years later in tandem with Davis after his own car had retired with carburetor trouble. After World War II, Rose claimed a controversial second Indy 500 when he ignored team orders and passed teammate Bill Holland in the 1947 race in a sleek, front-wheel drive Blue Crown Special. He bested Holland again in 1948 to win his third Indy 500 and the final Indy car victory of his career.

Wilbur Shaw

Shaw became the first driver to win consecutive Indianapolis 500s when he drove to victory in the 1939 and '40 races. Coupled with his win in the 1937 event, Shaw became the second three time winner of the race, joining Louis Meyer in that category. Like another great driver of his time—Mauri Rose—Shaw's ability transcended different types of equipment. His first success in Indy cars came in the waning days of the great front wheel drive, supercharged Millers. Later he drove a Miller Special converted to fit the 'Junk Formula' to victory at

Detroit and Bridgeville (PA) in 1930. Shaw earned his first Indy 500 win in 1937 after the AAA allowed supercharged engines back in the sport, and his back-to-back Indy 500 wins in 1939 and 1940 came at the wheel of a sophisticated Maserati 8CTF after the AAA adopted international Grand Prix rules in 1938.

Tom Sneva

The high school principal-turned-racing-driver was known as 'the Gas Man' for good reason: the only way Sneva raced was flat-out. The first driver to top the 200 and 210 mph marks at Indianapolis, Sneva scored a total of 13 victories in his Indy car career and won successive championships in 1977 and '78 with Penske Racing, taking the latter title in a winless season. However, Sneva would win many times in the next few years, including the 1983 Indianapolis 500. The following season he fell just short of a third Indy car title, battling Mario Andretti down to the wire for the PPG Cup before finally finishing second.

Danny Sullivan

The former waiter and New York City taxi driver bounced back and forth between Europe and the USA in everything from Formula One to the Can-Am before finding a home in Indy car racing. He scored his first wins with Shierson Racing in 1984, then moved to Penske where he rebounded from a 200 mph spin to win the 1985 Indianapolis 500. Three years later he claimed the PPG Cup on the strength of nine poles and four wins. He later drove for the Patrick, Galles-Kraco and PacWest teams, winning twice more to bring his career total to 17. He retired from competition in the wake of a serious accident at Michigan in 1995, and has since become one of television's top racing analysts.

Al Unser, Jr

His father and uncle were a tough act to follow, but Al Unser, Jr. was up to the challenge. After graduating from the dirt tracks of the Southwest to the Super Vee and Can-Am titles, he finished fifth in his Indy car debut in 1983 at age 20. Al, Jr. earned his first Indy car win in 1984, finished one point behind his father in the 1985 PPG Championship, then won the 1990 PPG Cup on the strength of six wins. After winning the 1992 Indy 500, he moved to Penske Racing and won eight races including the Indy 500 en route to the 1994 PPG Cup. He added four more wins in 1995—including an amazing sixth win in eight years at Long Beach—and ranks second among active drivers with 31 victories.

Bobby Unser

'Uncle Bobby' Unser battled his way to two Indy car titles and 35 wins in a career spanning three decades. Eldest of the second generation of racing Unsers, he competed in Mexican road races, sprint cars, and at Pike's Peak (winning no less than ten times) before his first Indy car race in 1963. He scored his first Indy 500 wins in 1968 on the way to his first title, then earned 15 poles in 21 races in 1971 and '72, and won his second title and Indy 500 with All American Racers. He moved to Penske Racing in 1979, and went on to a controversial third Indy 500 win—in which he 'passed' several cars while exiting the pits during a caution period. It would be the final win of his career.

Bill Vukovich

Bill Vukovich clawed his way from the California dirt tracks into the Indy car history books with a series of great drives at Indianapolis in the 1950s. The third driver to win back-to-back Indy 500s, Vukovich could easily have won four straight Memorial Day classics. He was leading the 1952 race when his steering failed nine laps from the finish. He dominated from start to finish in 1953 in brutally hot conditions and in 1954 he became the first driver to win the Indy 500 at an average speed of 130 mph. The following year Vukovich was in the running for another Indy 500 win when he lost control trying to avoid another accident, crashed and was killed instantly. His son Bill, Jr. and grandson both earned Rookie of the Year honors at Indianapolis, but Bill Vukovich III died in a racing accident in 1990.

DANNY SULLIVAN *From waiter to TV pundit by way of many daring feats—including taxi driving.*

BOBBY UNSER *Nine times winner at Pike's Peak before he even entered the Indy stakes.*

THE RACE

Blue Crown Special

The brainchild of former Indy car driver Lou Moore, the Blue Crown Special team won three straight Indy 500s to close-out the 1940s. After retiring from driving in 1937, Moore began building his Watteroth-Offies which won the 1938 and '41 Indy 500s. During World War II he began planning a new car, one which would take advantage of the high octane aviation gasoline introduced during the war, coupled with light weight, front wheel drive and an extraordinarily slippery shape.

In 1946 Moore secured sponsorship from the Blue Crown Spark Plug Company to finance his cars, and hired Mauri Rose and Bill Holland as drivers. Rose and Holland qualified third and eighth, respectively, for the 1947 Indy 500 and, following Moore's orders to drive at a conservative pace in order to take maximum advantage of their good fuel mileage and low tire wear (thanks to their light weight}, stayed in contention throughout the first half of the race. While the heavier, thirstier dirt track cars made two and three pit stops, the Blue Crown Specials needed just one stop. With Holland and Rose running 1-2 in the late stages of the race, Moore gave his drivers the 'EZ' sign, whereupon Rose promptly passed his teammate to take the win.

1948 was something of a case of *dêja vu*, as Rose again beat Holland to the checkered flag at Indy—albeit in a straight contest. Holland finally had his day when he averaged 121.327 mph to beat Johnnie Parsons' new Kurtis roadster to win the 1949 Indy 500. However, Holland's closest competition again came from Rose, who traded the lead with his team-mate during the race before falling out with a broken magneto eight laps shy of the finish.

Holland and Rose figured in the 1950 race as well, but this time Parsons' roadster had the legs of Blue Crown Specials, and when the race was stopped for rain after 345 miles Moore's three race winning streak came to a screeching halt as well. The roadster design would go on to dominate the Indianapolis 500 through the 1950s and into the early '60s.

TEAMS

Leader Card Racers

Bob Wilke rates as one of the legendary team owners/entrants of the roadster era that lasted from the early 1950s through the mid '60s. Milwaukee paper products company scion Wilke put his Leader Card team at the top of the heap in 1959 when he hired legendary designer/builder A.J. Watson to build two new roadsters plus a dirt car for driver Rodger Ward. Several years previously Watson had refined the roadster concept (where the engine was offset to the left of the chassis, resulting in a lower frontal area and improved weight distribution as compared to the traditional dirt cars) with his torsion bar suspended Zink Special which also featured a lighter but stronger frame than traditional chassis.

Ward took Watson's new Leader Card roadster to victory in the 1959 Indy 500 and went on to become national champion on the strength of additional victories at Milwaukee and in the team's dirt car at DuQuoin and in the Hoosier 100 at the Indiana State Fairgrounds. Ward and Leader Card Racers went on to two more national championships and more than a dozen wins— including a second Indy 500 triumph in 1962—in the next four years.

The partnership between Watson and the Leader Card team continued after the demise of the roadster, with Ward finishing second in the 1964 Indy 500 in a Watson-designed rear-engined machine. Bobby Unser enjoyed much of his early success with the Leader Card team, including his first Indy 500 victory and national championship in 1968.

Following Bob Wilke's death in 1970, his son Ralph continued Leader Card Racers' legacy under Watson's direction. Outstripped by the increasingly more well-financed teams such as Penske, Patrick and Newman/Haas in the 1980s, Wilke and Watson finally closed the doors on the Leader Card team at the conclusion of the 1994 season.

Team Lotus

A legendary combination in Formula One, Colin Chapman, Jimmy Clark and Lotus also made an indelible impact on Indy car racing in the 1960s. Chapman's innovative monocoque chassis had already revolutionized Grand Prix racing by the time he turned his attention to the Indianapolis 500 in 1963. Their sport dominated since the early 1950s by space framed, front-engined roadsters, the Indy car fraternity had watched in mild amusement when

1959/60 World Champion Jack Brabham drove his nimble (if underpowered) rear-engined Cooper-Climax to ninth place at the 1961 Indy 500.

Spurred on by Dan Gurney, who witnessed the promise rear-engined cars held at Indy and who was racing in Formula One at the time, Chapman entered into a partnership with Ford to build three Lotus 29 Indy cars for the 1963 race. Although a poor pit stop dropped Gurney from contention, Clark was within striking distance of leader Parnelli Jones' roadster in the closing stages of the race when Jones' car began leaking oil. Clark backed-off, certain Jones would either be black flagged

or blow up. In one of the more controversial decisions in Indy 500 history, officials opted not to black flag Jones and he won the race with Clark second.

Later that year, Clark took time off from Formula One to race the Lotus-Ford at Milwaukee and scored his first win in Indy car competition. The big prize, however, would prove elusive. Clark and Chapman returned to Indianapolis in 1964 and won the pole position. But although he led the race comfortably, Clark dropped out with suspension failure caused by chunking tires, and A.J. Foyt earned his second Indy 500 victory in a roadster.

By 1965 the Funny Car revolution was a *fait accompli*, with most of the

starting field at Indianapolis made up of rear engined chassis. Although he didn't win the pole, Clark dominated the Indianapolis 500 in his Lotus 34 and became the first driver to average more than 150 mph in winning the Memorial Day classic.

Clark and Lotus would return to Indianapolis in 1966, but finished second after a couple of spins (although Chapman long believed a scoring error cost them the race). Clark was an early retiree in 1967 and the following year he lost his life in a crash in a Formula Three race in Germany. Chapman returned to Indianapolis in 1968 and 1969 but Lotus was destined never to repeat its 1965 success.

PENNSYLVANIA INTERNATIONAL SPEEDWAY

Newman/Haas Racing

The partnership between one of America's leading racers and one of its leading actors has produced one of Indy car racing's most successful teams over the past fifteen years. Carl Haas, who used his successful race car importing business as the foundation for some of America's top sports car racing teams in the 1960s and '70s, joined forces with Academy Award-winning actor Paul Newman—himself a successful amateur racer—to form Newman/Haas Racing in 1983.

The third member of the triumvirate was Mario Andretti, who would go on to drive an unprecedented thirteen seasons with the team, winning the 1984 PPG Cup in the process. Like his great rival, Roger Penske, Haas dabbled in Formula One for a spell before focusing his team's energies in Indy car racing. As a result, Newman/Haas became one of the leading teams in Indy car racing, with Andretti scoring nine more wins before one of the more celebrated pairings in racing history came into being in 1989, when Michael Andretti joined the team.

Together, Mario and Michael Andretti formed a devastating one-two punch, with the senior Andretti's unparalleled technical expertise and experience augmented by his son's fierce aggression. 1991 saw Newman/Haas score eight wins and lead more than half the racing laps on the way to Michael Andretti's PPG Cup. The following year, Newman/Haas raced the new Ford/Cosworth XB engine to five more wins and lead an amazing 55.8% of the season's racing laps.

It was a tough act to follow, but with Michael Andretti off to Formula One in 1993, Newman/Haas signed-on reigning World Champion Nigel Mansell. The historic (if turbulent) partnership between Mansell and Mario Andretti saw the former win the team's third PPG Cup in impressive fashion, scoring five wins and seven poles, while the latter earned the 51st and final win of his Indy car career.

Michael Andretti subsequently returned to Newman/Haas in 1995 and, in keeping with the team's legacy of high profile pairings, was joined by another second generation driver; Christian Fittipaldi. In 1997, Haas severed a long-standing association with Lola Cars, Ltd. in order to enter into a partnership with Swift Engineering, long one of America's leading race car designers and builders.

NOVI/GRANATELLI: *After taking over the Novi team the Granatelli family developed the STP turbine pictured here.*

Novi/Granatelli Racing

Few racing cars have engendered the loyal following that the famed Novis enjoyed during the late 1940s and 1950s. Financed by Michigan businessman Lew Welch, the original supercharged Novi engine was designed by the Winfield brothers and installed in a streamlined chassis designed by Frank Curtis.

Entered for 1941 AAA champi-onship runner-up Ralph Hepburn in the 1946 Indy 500, the Novi wasn't ready to run until four days before the race. With the starting grid at Indianapolis set first by the day and then by the speed at which a car qual-ifies, the pole position had long since been won by Cliff Bergere at an average speed of 126.471 mph. His Novi engine shrieking along ahead of him, Hepburn uncorked a qualify-ing run of 133.944 mph to establish a record that still stands for the great-est discrepancy between the pole position and fastest qualifier.

In the race itself, Hepburn retired after 121 laps and a pattern was established. Blazingly fast (Hepburn topped 170 mph on the straight-aways at Indy) and earsplittingly loud, the Novis were unreliable and heavy—some 300 pounds heavier than the Blue Crown Specials. The Novis were destined never to win a race, the high water mark coming in 1948 when Duke Nalon finished third at Indianapolis.

Welch ultimately sold his team to Andy Granatelli in 1961. Ironically, Granatelli would later introduce the antithesis of the aurally impressive Novi when, in 1967, he took advan-tage of a loophole in the rules to enter a turbine-powered car at Indianapolis. Parnelli Jones drove away from the competition in the STP Turbine until a transmission bearing failed three laps from the finish. Although USAC subse-quently tightened its regulations regarding turbines, Granatelli returned to the Speedway with several new turbines, none of which finished the 1968 race. Granatelli would finally achieve success at Indianapolis when Mario Andretti scored his only Indy 500 win in 1969 in a Hawk-Ford pressed into service when he wrecked Granatelli's original entry—a Lotus-Ford—dur-ing practice.

Penske Racing

After a tentative entry into the sport in 1968, Penske Racing has become the most successful team in Indy car history. The statistics are impressive enough: nine Indy car titles, 96 race wins (including ten Indianapolis 500 victories) and 116 pole positions. The roster of Penske drivers past and present reads like a Who's Who of Indy car racing: the Unsers (Al, Bobby and Al, Jr.), Rick Mears, Danny Sullivan, Tom Sneva, Emerson Fittipaldi, Paul Tracy, Mark Donohue and, on occasion, Mario Andretti.

Ultimately, it is the standard of preparation and presentation emblematic of the organization's motto—Effort Equals Results—that have established Penske Racing as the standard by which all other Indy car teams are judged.

Penske Racing's origins date to the 1950s when Roger Penske raced his private sports car while attending college. Penske enjoyed considerable success as a driver, but retired in 1965 to focus on his business career. He became one of America's leading entrepreneurs and today the Penske Corporation's transportation services, automotive and performance divisions employ some 25,000 worldwide and have annualized revenues of $4 billion.

While fashioning his business empire, Penske established his team as a dominant force in American racing. Penske Racing won the United Road Racing Championship, the Can-Am, the Trans-Am and, in 1968, entered its first Indy 500. Donohue won the 1972 Indy 500 and, after a brief involvement in Formula One in which Donohue lost his life, Penske Racing concentrated on Indy cars. The team won its first Indy car titles in 1977 and '78 with Tom Sneva and went on to dominate the 1980s with Mears winning three titles, Al Unser two, and Danny Sullivan another.

Penske himself grew into a leading figure on the Indy car scene as, together with several other leading team owners including Pat Patrick, he helped organize the Championship Auto Racing Teams organization which broke away from the United States Auto Club to establish the PPG Indy Car World Series in 1979. Penske was also instrumental in the founding of Ilmor Engineering which, first in partnership with Chevrolet and more recently, Mercedes-Benz, produced some of the most successful engines in Indy car history, as evinced by the 1994 season in which Marlboro Penske Racing won 12 of 16 races. Long one of the only Indy car teams to build its own chassis, Penske Racing is also active in NASCAR racing with driver Rusty Wallace.

Duesenberg versus Miller

The Roaring Twenties are synonymous with board tracks, Ralph DePalma, Tommy Milton, Jimmy Murphy, Frank Lockhart ... and Duesenbergs and Millers. For the best part of a decade the creations of the brothers Duesenberg—Augie and Fred—and Harry Miller ruled the AAA National Championship. The Duesenbergs' first racing project came through their involvement in the Mason race car in 1912. By 1914 they were producing cars of their own and, later, engines for the Army Air corps during World War I. The innovative Miller first became involved with cars through the invention of his Master Carburetor and later worked for the Duesenbergs.

When the AAA downsized engines in the national championship in 1920 from 300 to 188 cubic inches, Miller struck out on his own. His first success came with a straight-8 engine based on a Duesenberg design, a design which had been unsuccessful in its original form but which Miller's meticulous production methods turned into a winner. Millers and Miller-powered Duesies dominated the 1922 and 1923 seasons, but the Duesenbergs responded with a new supercharger design that helped power their cars to victory in the 1924 Indianapolis 500, although Murphy won the national championship in a Miller.

Miller responded first with a supercharger design of his own. Later, he introduced a front-wheel drive car that would be the basis for the marque's domination in later years, although Peter DePaolo won the 1925 Indy 500 and the national title in a Duesie. In 1926, the AAA reduced the engine size to 91 cubic inches and Miller produced front and rear-wheel drive versions of his Miller 91. The Miller 91 completely dominated the latter half of the decade, winning all but three races before the AAA introduced the low-cost 'Junk Formula' in response to the hard economic times of the Depression.

The combination of the board tracks, the power and handling of the Millers—and the brave men who drove them—resulted in scores of records. In 1926, Lockhart lapped the Atlanta board track at 147 mph and in 1927 every race but the Indianapolis 500 was won at an average speed of 116 mph or better, while Millers set scores of land speed records as well.

THE RACE

Laguna Seca

One of the world's most challenging and photogenic natural terrain road courses, the story of Laguna Seca Raceway in many ways mirrors the growth of racing in America.

Constructed on the US Army's Fort Ord Reservation in the hills above California's scenic Monterey Peninsula in the 1950s, Laguna Seca (or dry lake) was the haunt of amateur racers for the better part of a decade before the SCCA's professional sports car series finally coalesced into the United States Road Racing Championship, and later, the Can-Am.

Originally 1.9 miles in length, Laguna Seca was unusual for a road course in that it ran counterclockwise and featured almost exclusively left hand turns, the first four of which were breathtakingly fast. The track was also noted for its dramatic elevation changes, most spectacularly illustrated in the famed Corkscrew Turn that consisted of a left-right-left esse bend dropping the equivalent of a five story building in 1/4 mile.

With the slow demise of the Can-Am, Laguna Seca and America's other leading road circuits such as Mid-Ohio and Road America were in need of another major event each summer. Looking to expand to new markets outside of Indy car racing's traditional oval track events, CART embraced the opportunity to go road racing in the 1980s.

The Laguna Seca Indy car race quickly became a favorite on the schedule, what with the challenging track, a scenic locale and the attractions of the central California coast close at hand. However, the Indy cars soon proved too much for the circuit, as lap times edged closer and closer to the 50 second mark. Thus circuit organizers undertook a major renovation in 1989 that saw a series of turns added to the 'infield' section of the track to bring the length up to 2.214 miles while retaining much of the original facility's character.

TRACKS

Long Beach

What began as little more than a pipe dream in the mind of English emigre Chris Pook has blossomed into one of Indy car racing's premier events. First held as a Formula 5000 race in 1974, the Long Beach Grand Prix helped re-awaken street course racing all over the world, sparked the renewal of an aging city and now attracts upwards of 300,000 souls every April.

Not bad for a race most experts said would never happen. It was in 1973 that Pook first conceived the idea of a race through the streets of Long Beach—then a dilapidated port city. Against all odds, Pook managed to convince the SCCA to hold a Formula 5000 race there in the fall of 1975. More incredible yet, six months later Long Beach hosted the US Grand Prix West Formula One race and the event was off and running. The following year Mario Andretti passed Jody Scheckter in the closing laps at Long Beach to become the first—and to date only American driver to win his home Grand Prix.

The event proved such a success that new street circuit events sprang up all over the world from Birmingham, England to Miami, Florida. But the rising costs associated with holding a Formula One race—coupled with Indy car racing's emerging popularity—led Pook to switch to the PPG Indy Car World Series in 1984.

He's never looked back. The success of Long Beach as an Indy car race paved the way for additional CART street circuit events, and today's PPG Series also includes races on the streets of Vancouver, Toronto, Detroit, and Surfers Paradise, Australia. The event also spawned a turnaround in the fortunes of Long Beach, and the race course is in a near-continual state of metamorphosis in order to accommodate the major construction projects reshaping the city.

Another feature of Long Beach is the success enjoyed by many of the sport's great names there over the years. It was once said your name had to be either Andretti or Unser to win at Long Beach. No wonder. Mario Andretti won three of the first four Indy car races there—Michael Andretti won the other. Then Al Unser, Jr. took four straight before Danny Sullivan finally broke the string in 1992—but he had to bump Unser out of the way to do it! Although Paul Tracy and Jimmy Vasser have since won at Long Beach, Unser won again in 1994 and '95 to stretch his remarkable record to six wins.

The Indianapolis Motor Speedway

Conceived in 1909 as a combination race track and automotive test facility, the Indianapolis Motor Speedway has become the world's most storied race track. Founded by Carl Fisher and three Indiana-based partners, the 2.5-mile rectangular oval featured four turns 1/4 mile in length and banked at 9 degrees, connected by two 5/8 mile straightaways and a pair of 1/8 mile straightaways or chutes.

Initially paved with a mix of tar and crushed stones, the Speedway was repaved with more than three million bricks after the original surface deteriorated during the facility's inaugural event, leading to a number of fatalities. The new brick surface prompted the circuit's nickname; 'the Brickyard.' After holding a series of sprint races in 1910, Fisher and his associates decided to hold a single 500 mile race on Memorial Day beginning in 1911.

The first Indy 500 was won by Ray Harroun, who wheeled his Marmon Wasp to victory at an average speed of 74.602 mph before some 80,000 spectators. Subsequently, the Indianapolis Motor Speedway became the center of racing in the United States and the Indy 500 became the most famous race in America. Even amidst the Great Depression, when the AAA championship shrank to two or three races, the Indy 500 remained one of the leading events on the sports calendar.

During World War II, however, the facility fell into a terrible state of disrepair until local businessman Tony Hulman purchased the track in 1945. The Speedway—parts of which had been repaved with asphalt beginning in 1937—re-opened for business in 1946 and, over the next three decades, Hulman's constant investment turned the track into one of the world's great sports facilities, with some 250,000 permanent seats.

Although the Hulman family retained control of the Speedway following Tony's death in 1977, the track was administered by a succession of presidents, including John Cooper and Joe Cloutier. In 1989, Hulman's grandson Tony George was named president of the Indianapolis Motor Speedway. Under George's direction, IMS introduced a second major event to its schedule in 1995—the Brickyard 400 NASCAR race. Dissatisfied with the direction Indy car racing had taken under the auspices of Championship Auto Racing Teams, George also established the rival Indy Racing League in 1996.

Rio de Janeiro

The inaugural Rio 400, staged in 1996, was not Indy car racing's first trip outside North America; it wasn't even Indy car racing's first trip to South America. But it was one of the most significant races in the sport's history.

Staged on a trapezoidal 'oval' built on the former site of the Brazilian Grand Prix, the Rio 400 was the fulfillment of the dreams of Emerson Fittipaldi, whose Indy car success sparked a surge in the sport's popu-larity throughout Latin America.

Before Fittipaldi came to Indy car racing, the PPG Indy Car World Series was hardly even a national sport for 364 days a year. True, on the 365th day much of the auto racing world focused on the Indianapolis 500. But a minute portion of that Memorial Day attention carried over to the traditional Indy 500 follow-up race at Milwaukee; less still to other races.

CART's drive to establish the Indy car series as a big league sport—rather than just an appetizer for the Indy 500—helped make the sport a national entity. Fittipaldi's first Indy car win in 1985 and subsequent championship in 1989 put the sport on the international radar screen.

For years Fittipaldi worked with businesses, government and local organizers to put together an Indy car race in Brazil. But the lack of a suitable facility was always a road-block; so too was the Federation Internationale de Sport Automobile's belief that Indy car racing was threatening Formula One's popularity.

The issue came to a head when CART staged a street race in Surfers Paradise, Australia, in 1991. The FISA threatened to revoke the participants' international licenses, but relented after reaching a compromise that saw CART agree to limit future 'off-shore' races to oval tracks.

The Rio 400 was the first of these races. The track—named 'The Emerson Fittipaldi Speedway at Nelson Piquet International Raceway'—resembled a four-cornered road course more than an 'oval.' But 100,000 Brazilians came out to see what all the fuss was about and went home delighted when favorite son Andre Ribeiro edged Al Unser, Jr. for the win. With a race slated for Japan's Twin Ring Motegi in 1998 and talk of an event in Europe before the millennium, Indy car racing's international future seems assured.

's Peak

Climbing to an altitude of 14,110 feet on a twisting 12.4 mile dirt road, the Pike's Peak Hillclimb was a fixture on the national championship calendar from 1947–1955 and from 1965–1969. Although Mario Andretti won the hillclimb in its final year as a national championship event, the Unser family dominated Pike's Peak through the years, with Bobby scoring thirteen class wins and ten overall victories on the mountain during his career.

Board Tracks

An offshoot of the pre-automobile bicycle tracks constructed entirely of wood and paved with 2" by 4" planks, board tracks were among the early alternatives to the dirt tracks and road courses of the early 1900s. The first board track built with motor racing in mind was a circular track constructed in 1910 at Playa del Ray near Los Angeles, featuring some three million feet of 2x4s on the 45 foot wide, one mile track, banked at 20 degrees. William Endicott won the first event at Playa del Ray at an average speed of 66.2 mph, and before long board tracks were popping up all over the country, from Tacoma to Atlantic City and from Beverly Hills to Miami.

The board tracks increased in popularity after World War I, and in the 1920s virtually all of the AAA championship races—save for the Indianapolis 500—were contested on board tracks ranging from half a mile to two miles in length. The heyday of the board tracks coincided with the climax of the competition between the Duesenberg and Miller teams, and the sight (and sound) of fleets of Duesies and Millers racing around the high-banked board tracks was truly a spectacle to behold. Frank Lockhart won a race at the 1.25 mile Charlotte track in November of 1926 at an average speed of 132.40 mph—it was not until Sam Hanks won the 1957 Indy 500 at more than 135 mph that Lockhart's record was broken in championship competition.

Unfortunately, high maintenance costs, coupled with the crippling economic forces of the Great Depression, brought an end to the board tracks era. The tracks developed splinters that were equally lethal to drivers and tires alike—as well as potholes through which adventurous spectators would poke their heads for a uniquely dangerous view of the action. Some tracks simply rotted away, others burned to the ground while still more were dismantled, with some of the wood salvaged—for use in housing developments.

Dirt Tracks

Dirt tracks played a crucial role in the development and lore of Indy car racing. From the inception of the AAA national championship in 1909, which included two races at an Indianapolis Motor Speedway still coated in its original mixture of tar and crushed stones, through the halcyon days of the 1950s when the AAA and USAC schedules were so dominated by dirt tracks that teams built one car specifically for the Indy 500 and others for the dirt track part of the schedule, dirt tracks were an integral feature of Indy car racing.

The impact of dirt tracks on the sport waned during the heyday of the board tracks in the 1920s. More recently, the increasingly specialized nature of the sport has seen dirt tracks eliminated from the Indy car schedule since the 1971 season.

The attraction of a quarter, half and one mile dirt ovals was two fold. For the track owner and promoter, construction and maintenance expense were a fraction of the cost involved in building, paving—and repaving—the board tracks of the 1920s or the asphalt and concrete tracks of the '50s, '60s and today.

But for drivers and fans alike, dirt track racing offers a uniquely exciting challenge. The nature of the surface enables drivers to slide their cars through the turns, while its complex and ever-changing consistency often results in more than one fast line through the turns; or a fast line that changes location during the course of the event.

The most celebrated dirt tracks on the Indy car schedule included the mile ovals at Sacramento, Phoenix, the Indiana State Fairgrounds, the Wisconsin state Fair Park, Langhorne Speedway and Syracuse. But the advent of modern paving techniques—coupled with the hope of drawing increased number of fans lured by the prospects of going home without taking a large part of the race track with them, prompted more and more tracks to switch to pavement. By the mid 1960s, the USAC championship featured but a handful of dirt tracks, and in 1970 Al Unser became the last driver to win a championship event on dirt when he won the 100 mile race at Sacramento.

STATISTICS

HEAD AND SHOULDERS... *Mario Andretti's successful career is evident from his statistics.*

CAREER WINS

1.	A.J. Foyt	67
2.	Mario Andretti	52
3.	Al Unser	39
4.	Michael Andretti	35
	Bobby Unser	35
6.	Al Unser, Jr.	31
7.	Rick Mears	29
8.	Johnny Rutherford	27
9.	Rodger Ward	26
10.	Gordon Johncock	25
11.	Ralph DePalma	24
	Bobby Rahal	24
13.	Tommy Milton	23
14	Tony Bettenhausen	22
	Emerson Fittipaldi	22
16.	Earl Cooper	20
17.	Jimmy Bryan	19
	Jimmy Murphy	19
19.	Ralph Mulford	17
	Danny Sullivan	17

LAPS LED (1946-1996)

1.	Mario Andretti	7585
2.	A.J. Foyt	6621
3.	Al Unser	5812
4.	Michael Andretti	5219
5.	Bobby Unser	4862
6.	Rick Mears	3506
7.	Gordon Johncock	3417
8.	Al Unser, Jr.	3035
9.	Bobby Rahal	2968
10.	Rodger Ward	2955

POLE POSITIONS (1930-1996)

1.	Mario Andretti	67
2.	A.J. Foyt	53
3.	Bobby Unser	49
4.	Rick Mears	38
5.	Michael Andrettti	30
6.	Al Unser	27
7.	Johnny Rutherford	23
8.	Gordon Johncock	20
9.	Rex Mays	19
	Danny Sullivan	19

YEAR BY YEAR NATIONAL CHAMPIONS 1909-1996

1909	George Robertson	1930	Billy Arnold
1910	Ray Harroun	1931	Louis Schneider
1911	Ralph Mulford	1932	Bob Carey
1912	Ralph DePalma	1933	Louis Meyer
1913	Earl Cooper	1934	Bill Cummings
1914	Ralph DePalma	1935	Kelly Petillo
1915	Earl Cooper	1936	Mauri Rose
1916	Dario Resta	1937	Wilbur Shaw
1917	Earl Cooper	1938	Floyd Roberts
1918	Ralph Mulford	1939	Wilbur Shaw
1919	Howard Wilcox	1940	Rex Mays
1920*	Tommy Milton	1941	Rex Mays
	Gaston Chevrolet	1946	Ted Horn
1921	Tommy Milton	1947	Ted Horn
1922	Jimmy Murphy	1948	Ted Horn
1923	Eddie Hearne	1949	Johnnie Parsons
1924	Jimmy Murphy	1950	Henry Banks
1925	Peter DePaolo	1951	Tony Bettenhausen
1926	Harry Hartz	1952	Chuck Stevenson
1927	Peter DePaolo	1953	Sam Hanks
1928	Louis Meyer	1954	Jimmy Bryan
1929	Louis Meyer	1955	Bob Sweikert

* AAA records regarding the 1920 national championship are inconclusive. By one account, the series championship consisted of five races; by another the championship included 11 events. Chevrolet won the five race championship; Milton the eleven race championship.

THE WINNER *A.J. Foyt streaks to the finish in the 1967 Indy 500.*

CHAMPION

MILLER GENUINE DRAFT 200

JUNE 3, 1990

WISCONSIN STATE FAIR PARK SPEEDWAY

Statistics

USAC

1956	Jimmy Bryan
1957	Jimmy Bryan
1958	Tony Bettenhausen
1959	Rodger Ward
1960	A.J. Foyt
1961	A.J. Foyt
1962	Rodger Ward
1963	A.J. Foyt
1964	A.J. Foyt
1965	Mario Andretti
1966	Mario Andretti
1967	A.J. Foyt
1968	Bobby Unser
1969	Mario Andretti
1970	Al Unser
1971	Joe Leonard
1972	Joe Leonard
1973	Roger McCluskey
1974	Bobby Unser
1975	A.J. Foyt
1976	Gordon Johncock
1977	Tom Sneva
1978	Tom Sneva
1979**	A.J. Foyt

** The United States Auto Club and Championship Auto Racing Teams ran separate championships in 1979.

See page 186 for CART listings.

SPEED 3 *Arie Luyendyk has the third fastest race speed.*

CLOSEST FINISHES

Date	Track	Distance Margin	Winner
4/10/21	Beverly Hills	25 miles .02s	Ralph DePalma
4/10/21	Beverly Hills	25 miles .04s	Jimmy Murphy
5/24/92	Indianapolis	500 miles .043s	Al Unser, Jr.
2/25/23	Beverly Hills	25 miles .05s	Jimmy Murphy
7/30/95	Michigan	500 miles .056s	Scott Pruett

FASTEST RACES

Date	Race	Average Speed	Winner
8/6/90	Michigan 500	189.727mph	Al Unser, Jr.
8/1/93	Michigan 500	188.203mph	Nigel Mansell
5/27/90	Indianapolis 500	185.981mph	Arie Luyendyk
9/18/83	Michigan 200	182.325mph	Rick Mears
9/30/79	Atlanta 150	182.094mph	Rick Mears
10/6/73	Texas 200	181.918mph	Gary Bettenhausen
9/28/96	Michigan 250	181.701mph	Bobby Rahal
8/7/88	Michigan 500	180.654mph	Danny Sullivan
8/26/73	Ontario 100	179.910mph	Wally Dallenbach
8/2/92	Michigan 500	177.625mph	Scott Goodyear

TWINS *Al Unser Jr (left) and Rick Mears (above) are closely matched in the records.*

101

DRAG RACING

The basic premise of drag racing seems very simple: accelerate in a straight line from a standing start and get to the finish before the other guy. What could be simpler? From the time that prehistoric men raced each other for mammoth kills to the pre-Olympics foot races of ancient Greece, to Roman chariot races, the object has always been the same: get there first and claim the prize.

Centuries after ancient Rome, Ben Hur's four-horsepower chariot no longer is the fastest set of wheels in town. On quarter-mile dragstrips around the world, the thundering hoofbeats of 5,000-horsepower behemoths, drunk on an exotic blend of $30-per-gallon nitromethane fuel and supercharged air, rend the atmosphere and assault the senses with the thunder of a veritable bottled dynamite that helps propel these modern chariots from zero to 100 mph in less than a second—faster than a jumbo jet, a fighter jet, or an F1 race car—and to 320 mph in four and a half seconds.

Championship drag racing in the 1990s is a multimillion-dollar spectacle of high drama and high power played out before millions of race fans at sprawling stadium-like racing facilities worldwide, and to hundreds of millions on television.

The National Hot Rod Association's championship series, encompassing more than 20 events each with a purse in excess of a million dollars and a championship purse fund of more than $2 million, is the home to the sport's biggest sponsors, brightest stars, and best performances.

NHRA drag racing was born on the back roads and dry lake beds of Southern California more than 40 years ago and grew up under the guidance of NHRA founder Wally Parks. With the vision of Parks and those around him, NHRA drag racing has become one of the world's most popular and successful forms of motorsports.

Rival sanctioning bodies like the American Hot Rod Association (AHRA), which was founded in 1958 and folded in 1984, and the International Hot Rod Association (IHRA), founded in 1971 and still alive in America's Deep South, offered their own unique variety of classes and local stars to compete with NHRA's highly polished act.

Drag racing offers a wide array of classes to fit just about every type of vehicle with almost any imaginable powerplant, from the exotic tube-framed, nitro-burning Top Fuelers and Funny Cars to near-stock sedans with four cylinder engines that would be right at home on the highway.

Drivers work hard to hone their skills, developing hair-trigger reactions and a oneness with their machine. The sport attracts all types of competitors, from wealthy businessmen with high-dollar, rolling-garage transporters and mega-dollar corporate sponsorships to the hobbyist, who packs the wife and kids into the back of the car, hitches up the trailer, and is at the track and home over the span of a weekend, all on money saved by clipping grocery coupons.

Both the princes and the paupers, though, seek the same truth: who has the fastest set of wheels in town?

SPEED KINGS *Of all the modern-day chariot drivers none has had more NHRA wins than Joe Amato.*

THE HISTORY

IT'S A DRAG *Although no one seems to know where the term 'drag racing' came from, everyone agrees that it has long been one of America's most exciting motor sports.*

Stars of the future *Bracket racing is where the next generation of racers cut their teeth.*

Although the tiretracks of its history are clear, the origin of the term 'drag racing' is not. The theories are almost as many and varied as the machines that have populated its ranks for five decades. Explanations range from a simple challenge ('Drag your car out of the garage and race me!') to geographical locale (the 'main drag' was a city's main street, often the only one wide enough to accommodate two vehicles), to the mechanical (to 'drag' the gears meant to hold the transmission in gear longer than normal). Whatever its origination, drag racing in the 1990s brings to mind another term: success story.

Born on the backroads of America in the post World War II years, drag racing's roots were planted on dry lake beds like Muroc in California's Mojave Desert, where hot rodders had congregated since the early 1930s and speeds first topped 100 mph.

The Southern California Timing Association's first 'Speed Week,' held at the famed Bonneville Salt Flats in 1949, was the result of a dilligent effort by Wally Parks, then SCTA's executive secretary. It was here that racers first began running 'against the clock'—actually, a stopwatch—coaxing their vehicles to accelerate quicker rather than trying simply to attain high top speeds.

The first drag strip, the Santa Ana Drags, began running on an airfield in Southern California in 1950, and quickly gained popularity among the Muroc crowd because of its revolutionary computerized speed clocks.

When Parks became editor of the monthly enthusiast magazine Hot Rod, he had the forum and the power to form the National Hot Rod Association in 1951 to 'create order from chaos' by instituting safety rules and performance standards that helped legitimize the sport. He was its first president.

NHRA held its first official race in April 1953, on a slice of the Los Angeles County Fairgrounds parking lot in Pomona, California. Four decades later, that track has undergone a $6 million expansion and renovation and hosts the NHRA season-opening Winternationals and the season finale, the Winston Finals. The aggressive upgrading of facilities to 'stadium' quality, with fan amenities, VIP towers, and tall grandstands, is the passion of NHRA President Dallas Gardner, who took the reins in 1984 when Parks became Board Chairman.

Now in its fifth decade, the NHRA is the world's largest motorsports sanctioning body, with more than 85,000 members, 144 member tracks, 32,000 licensed competitors, and nearly 4,000 member-track events. Nearly 150 companies participate in the industry's most comprehensive contingency program, posting more than $20 million in awards.

Attendance in 1996 exceeded one million for the tenth consecutive year, as more than 1.8 million fans enjoyed the 19-race series. The NHRA schedule expanded to 22 national events in 1997.

Those who can't make it to the races can watch them on television, as every NHRA national event is now broadcast on either network or cable television channels. More than 200 million viewers watched in 1996.

NHRA's partner in producing the world's fastest motor races is the R.J. Reynolds Tobacco Company, which has sponsored the championship purse through its Winston brand since 1975. That support has grown consistently, surpassing $1 million in 1988, and the addition in 1995 of the Winston Top 10 bonus program for professional competitors in the top 10 in the point standings at each national event increased R.J. Reynolds' support to $2.1 million.

Top Fuel and Funny Car season champions each earn $200,000, the Pro Stock champion $125,000, and the Pro Stock Motorcycle champion $30,000.

These vehicles are the stars of the sport and draw crowds of rabid fans to watch them practically defy the laws of nature. The nitromethane-powered engines of Top Fuel dragsters and Funny Cars produce more than 5,500 horsepower, about 40 times that of the average street car.

Like almost all racing cars, they have undergone tremendous evolution as racers upgraded,

experimented, theorized, and tested their equipment.

The first 'dragsters' were little more than street cars with lightly warmed-over engines and bodies chopped down to reduce weight. Eventually, professional chassis builders constructed purpose-built cars, bending and welding together tubing and planting the engine in the traditional spot, just in front of the driver; the engines, and the fuels they burned, became more exotic, more powerful, and, naturally, more temperamental.

Safety and innovation paved the way to rear-engined Top Fuel cars in the early 1970s, and once drag racing legend Don Garlits—himself a victim of the front-engined configuration when his transmission, which was nestled between his feet, exploded in 1970, severing half of his right foot—perfected the design, the sport never looked back. Today's Top Fuel dragsters are computer-designed wonders with sleek profiles and wind-tunnel-tested rear airfoils that exert 5,000 pounds of downforce on the rear tires with minimal aerodynamic drag.

As racers became smarter, the speed barriers fell: 260 mph toppled in 1984; 270 in 1986; 280 in 1987; 290 in 1989; and the magic 300 mph barrier fell before the wheels of former Funny Car champion Kenny Bernstein on March 20, 1992. Performances are clocked with precision timing equipment capable of measuring elapsed times to the thousandth of a second.

A modern Top Fueler, powered by an expensive all-aluminum Chrysler Hemi-replica engine, can accelerate from 0 to 100 mph in about 0.9 seconds; that's almost 11 seconds quicker than a Porsche 911 Turbo. These cars, which weigh just over 2,000 pounds, can exceed 260 mph in just 660 feet and nearly 320 mph at the end of the quarter-mile run while subjecting the driver to 5Gs of acceleration. Twin braking parachutes exert up to 5 negative Gs to help stop the cars past the finish line.

The 500-cubic-inch engines are a far cry from stock. Their aluminum blocks are topped with billet cylinder heads and a belt-driven supercharger that crams a mix of nitro, upwards of 95 percent, methanol, and air into the cylinders; a high-powered ignition system fires the charge, creating the power that is fed through an intricate clutch system directly to the rear end (there is no transmission), and on to the huge rear Goodyear tires.

With a dragster chassis and fuel-burning engine cloaked in a fiberglass replica of a production-car body, the Funny Cars—initially so called in the 1970s because of their wildly altered wheelbases and contorted body lines—traditionally perform within a half-second and 10 mph of their dragster brethren.

The Pro Stock cars must maintain exact-to-template bodylines and standard driver configuration, yet are capable of 200-mph speeds and six-second elapsed times with a 1,200-horsepower gasoline-burning 500-cubic-inch engine and a five speed transmission. The engines are fed by huge twin four-barrel carburetors mounted atop a custom-made sheetmetal intake manifold.

Pro Stock motorcycles feature highly modified four-cylinder Kawasaki or Suzuki powerplants displacing a maximum of 1,500 cubic centimeters. The high-revving engines reach 13,500 rpm and produce about 275 horsepower, enough to propel them to quarter-mile elapsed times in the 7.2-second range at speeds approaching 190 mph!

Alcohol-fueled dragsters and Funny Cars are at the top of the second tier of race cars, the sportsman competitors. Though most are hobby racers who split time between home, work, and the racetrack, some live off their winnings and sponsorship money. NHRA offers eight categories of competition: Alcohol Dragster, Alcohol Funny Car, Competition, Super Stock, Stock, Super Comp, Super Gas, and Super Street that provide a level of competition, technical ability, and affordability for just about any interested racer.

Drag racing also offers the opportunity for any licensed driver to take his or her street car out to the local track and compete on a handicap-start basis against other street cars. This 'bracket racing'—so named because the cars are classified by elapsed-time brackets—is where tomorrow's stars cut their teeth and learn the skills necessary to make the leap to official NHRA competition and the opportunity to drag their cars out and drag the gears with the legends of the sport.

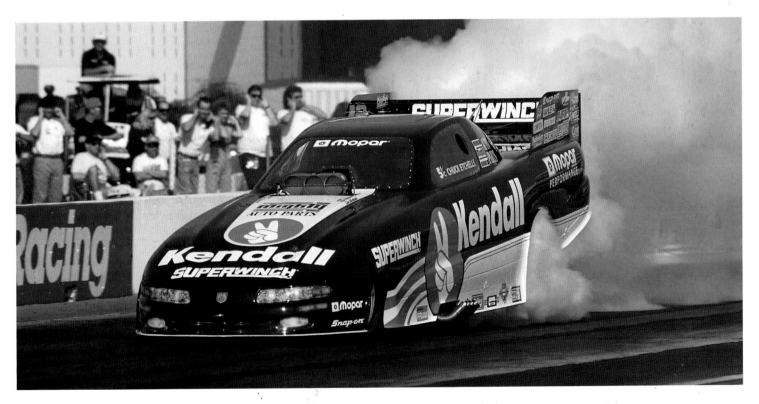

LEFT: LONG RIDERS *John Zookeeper in his 1970s Top Fueler* **ABOVE: BIG BUSINESS** *Millions of fans flock each year to view cars such as Chuck Etchells' Kendall Funny Car.*

AMATO THE GREAT

Drag racing icon 'Big Daddy' Don Garlits may be the most famous and revered Top Fuel racer to ever bury his talented foot on the throttle of a Top Fuel dragster, but he's not the winningest driver in the history of the NHRA, drag racing's premiere sanctioning body. That honor goes to the pride of Old Forge, Pa.— Joe Amato.

NHRA's first five-time champion, Amato won season titles in 1984, 1988, and an unprecedented three straight from 1990-92, and owns two more NHRA championships than Garlits. Amato's victory in 1996 at the season-ending Winston Select Finals also gave him one more win than Garlits, and he opened the 1997 season with two more victories, pushing his total to 38.

Amato, an avid, near-par golfer adored by his fans for his quirky superstitions and outlandish celebration rituals, has been a consistent threat in Top Fuel since graduating to the head of drag racing's class in 1982 following several years in an alcohol-fueled dragster, where he won three event titles. Amato has finished in the top ten of NHRA standings for 15 straight years since making the move to Top Fuel.

Amato, owner of Keystone Automotive Warehouse in Exeter, Pa., the largest auto parts chain on the American East Coast, has also won the prestigious Budweiser Classic, a high-dollar bonus race for the season's eight most consistent qualifiers, six times, and has broken numerous performance barriers. In 1984, the year of his first NHRA championship, his revolutionary high-winged dragster, tuned as it was for all five championship seasons by Tim Richards, was the first to break 260 mph and a few years later he was the first to top 280 mph. In 1996, he became the first driver to record a 4.5-second elapsed time with a 4.59 clocking at the Western Auto Nationals in Topeka, Kansas.

DRIVERS

Long before he won his first national-event title, at the 1986 Cajun Nationals, everyone already knew that Pat Austin was destined for greatness.

The son of 1960s fuel coupe racer Walt Austin displayed an uncanny cool and a knack for wheeling the family's Alcohol Funny Car that belied his 22 years of age. With the backing of his father's successful chain of Washington-state-based radiator and muffler shops, the never-ending hard work of his older brother, Mike, and the support of his mother, Sharon, they became an unstoppable force, winning NHRA championships in 1987, 1988, 1990, and 1991. In those five years, he competed in 78 NHRA national events and made the final round an amazing 57 times. Even more amazing was that in those 57 chances, he left empty-handed only 14 times. He was the low qualifier 28 times, set low e.t. 34 times, and top speed 37 times while amassing an incredible 222-35 win-loss record (86.3 percent).

As if the legend of Pat Austin needed it, he found a way to further imprint his name in the NHRA record books. When his Castrol GTX teammate Gary Ormsby fell terminally ill with cancer in 1991, the Austins bought his Top Fuel operation and, with but a few passes under their belts, qualified at the prestigious US Nationals. Austin drove both cars, won the Alcohol Funny Car title for the fourth straight time, and came within a bungled burnout of winning the Top Fuel title. Austin exploded his supercharger on the burnout, then watched dejectedly as Kenny Bernstein smoked the tires on his single pass. Frustrated by a driving error caused only by inexperience, Austin vowed not only to win in the fuel dragster before the season was out, but to win in both cars at the same event. It took him exactly two weeks to fulfill that gutsy call, winning both classes at the Sears Craftsman Nationals.

The Austins' stay in Top Fuel was short but earned them four more wins while Pat captured 14 more Alcohol Funny Car victories, giving him a combined total of 62 victories, second only to Pro Stock legend Bob Glidden.

BERNSTIEN

Kenny Bernstein will go down in history as the first driver to break the 300mph barrier.

Kenny Bernstein has accomplished a lot in a racing career that began more than 30 years ago, but his name will forever be etched into the history books as the last driver to break a significant mile-per-hour barrier. Bernstein was a four-time NHRA Funny Car champ (1985-89) before returning to his 1960s Top Fuel roots in 1990, and in 1996 became the first driver to win the championship in both fuel classes when he captured the NHRA Top Fuel championship. But it was March 20, 1992, that people will never forget. It was then that Bernstein became the first driver to break the 300-mph barrier with a speed of 301.70 mph at Gainesville Raceway in Gainesville, Florida, during the NHRA Gatornationals.

Bernstein, who financed his first Funny Car, the Chelsea King, with profits from his 16-store Chelsea Street Pub restaurant chain, long has been recognized as drag racing's most successful businessman, entrepreneur, and sponsorship acquirer, and at one time also fielded a NASCAR and IndyCar team concurrently with his Top Fuel operation. Bernstein has been sponsored by Budweiser since 1980, the second-longest alliance in motorsports, behind that enjoyed by Richard Petty and STP. That sponsorship paved the way for many other corporate sponsors in the 1980s and 1990s.

Entering the 1997 season, Bernstein was the fifth-winningest pro driver in NHRA history with 46 wins in 77 finals; 30 of those wins and 48 of the final were in Funny Car, where he is the sport's third-most successful driver, with the balance in Top Fuel.

In his 1996 championship season, he added four wins in seven final-round appearances, and reasserted his King of Speed reputation with a class-high clocking of 318.69 mph at the Chief Nationals in his native Texas.

There is no more popular drag racer today, perhaps ever, than Funny Car titan John Force. The Elvis Presley fanatic, who swore "I saw Elvis at 1,000 feet" after his accident at the 1992 Mid-South Nationals in Memphis, is a former truck driver who made it much better than good.

B lessed with the gift of gab that has landed him lucrative sponsorships and a loyal and large fan base, Force not only talks a good game: He's one of the sport's best drivers, able to deftly backpedal his smoking tires and thread the needle down any race course regardless of what his powerful mount has decided to do.

Much as Joe Amato's histrionics give him a statistical edge over Top Fuel legend Don Garlits, Force has also begun to overshadow Funny Car's leading man, Don Prudhomme, Force's lifelong hero.

In 1996, Force made NHRA history when he became its first six-time nitro champion, adding a dominating season in which he won an NHRA-record 13 times to previous season championships in 1990, 1991, 1993, 1994, and 1995. Force's vaunted Castrol GTX-sponsored Pontiac Firebird won 13 of the 16 final rounds and 65 of the 71 rounds it appeared in over the course of the 19-race series, and won the championship by more than 600 points, equivalent to Prudhomme's dominating 1976 season when he won the championship by more than 6,000 points under NHRA's old scoring system.

Force, who began racing Funny Cars in 1978 but did not earn his first victory until mid-1987, finished 1996 with 61 career wins in 95 final-round appearances, making him the winningest Funny Car driver in NHRA history. Force, second in career wins to Bob Glidden, who has 85, nonetheless is the winningest NHRA competitor of the 1990s with 56 victories. He has won at least 50 rounds every season since 1993, a feat unmatched by any driver during that time.

Force's 1996 efforts earned him the prestigious Driver of the Year award in balloting by nationwide motorsports media, the first drag racer to ever win the award.

111

GARLITS

Master innovator. Inveterate tinkerer. Horsepower king. Super strategist. Natural driver. Born leader. Barrier breaker. Versatile champion. Pick an adjective—they all apply to Donald Glenn Garlits, drag racing's 'Big Daddy.'

His is the name that even the non-sports fan knows. Everyone has heard of 'Big Daddy' Don Garlits, and his rise to fame was as fast as his race cars. From proprietor of Don's Garage, where in 1956 you could get your brakes adjusted for $2, to national motorsports hero less than a decade later, Garlits conquered the fans the way he vanquished his foes on the track: decisively.

After dominating racing in the southeast in the early 1960s, he accepted the challenge from a group of disbelieving Californians to come west, and the rest is history. His list of firsts and his accomplishments could easily fill this book. In 1957, he became the first driver to break the 170-mph barrier. He was also the first to surpass 180 in 1958, 200 in 1964, 240 in 1968, 250 in 1973, and 270 mph in 1986 in his line of predominately black 'Swamp Rat' Top Fuelers, almost all of them built by his own hand.

Following an accident with his front-engined Swamp Rat 13 in 1970 that severed half his right foot, Garlits refined the rear-engined design still in use today. His other innovations included bicycle front tires (1955), extended wheelbase chassis (1957), air spoilers (1963), port-injection system (1965), four-disc clutch system (1978), a turbine-powered car (1983), front ground effects (1985), and airplane-style wheels and modern streamlined body (1986).

Until he retired in 1992, Garlits was widely feared for his ability not only to outpower the competition, but outsmart them, too. His legendary skills carried him to 17 national championships (10 in AHRA, 4 in IHRA, and 3 in NHRA) and 112 event titles (51 in AHRA, 35 in NHRA, and 26 in IHRA). His back-to-back NHRA championships in 1983 and 1984 marked the first time that any racer had accomplished such a feat.

Drag racing's winningest driver, Pro Stock legend Bob Glidden was a winner from the time he debuted in the class. He won his first of a record 85 NHRA national-event titles at the 1973 US Nationals, exactly one year after taking his first runner-up in his first of a record 122 final-round appearances in his first start, at the 1972 US Nationals.

Glidden has dominated Pro Stock racing on three separate occasions, winning his titles in 1974-75, 1978-80, and 1985-89; the latter streak of five consecutive championships is also an NHRA record.

Glidden, a former Ford line mechanic and Stock and Super Stock racer, has won more championships—10—than any other NHRA Pro-class competitor; no other pro competitor has won more than the six owned by Funny Car powerhouse John Force, who has won the last four championships from 1993-1996 and is threatening to tie Glidden's consecutive championship streak.

Glidden has dominated drag racing's biggest race, the US Nationals in his homestate of Indianapolis, like no other racer. He didn't miss a final from 1977, when he was runner-up to Don Nicholson, through 1989, when he runner-upped to Larry Morgan. Glidden did win seven of the 11, which, when combined with his titles in 1973 and 1974, add up to a record nine Indy wins.

Glidden, who was elected to Motorsports Hall of Fame of America in 1994, had won at least one NHRA national event every year except two (1994 and 1996) since 1973 and finished in the top five of NHRA point standings for 16 consecutive seasons from 1977-92 and in the top ten 23 consecutive times—both NHRA records. Glidden became the first to win 50 national events at the Chief Auto Parts Nationals in Texas in 1986 and the first to win 75 three years later at the Pioneer Electronics Keystone Nationals in Pennsylvania. Glidden's final national-event victory was at the 1995 Mopar Parts Nationals in New Jersey, where he downed Jim Yates.

JOHNSON

People don't call Pro Stock racer Warren Johnson 'the Professor' just because of his scholarly demeanor, though he looks like he would be right at home in front of a chalkboard at any university. Johnson earned his scholarly sobriquet for his undying thirst for knowledge about the internal combustion engine: how it works and how to make it work better.

While racing as a 'weekend warrior' in his homestate of Minnesota, Johnson took night classes in engineering while working full-time in a metal fabrication shop. Although he remains just a few classes shy of a degree, Johnson soon began to put those skills to work in the real world, building race cars and engines. This business eventually provided him the capital to build a Pro Stock car in the early 1970s, and Johnson again found himself back in school: the school of racing hard knocks.

It took a lot of hard work and late hours and until the early 1980s for Johnson to establish himself as a threat in the competi-tive class. He won his first Pro Stock race in 1982, the same year that his Olds Starfire, the first of many cars in a long partnership with Oldsmobile, became the first Pro Stock car to eclipse 180 mph; four years later, Johnson became the first to surpass 190 and in late April 1997 testing broke drag racing's last great barrier, a 200 mph Pro Stock run, with a pass of 200.13 mph at the

Pennzoil Nationals in Virginia.

Since that first win, Johnson won 53 more times through the end of the 1996 season to rank as the third winningest Professional driver in NHRA history. After six championship runner-ups through the years, WJ, as he is known to his legions of fans, finally won his first NHRA championship in 1992 and then went on to win it again the next year and yet again in 1995, all in Oldsmobile Cutlass entries that are now viewed as rolling mechanical marvels and trendsetters.

Shirley Muldowney's life story reads like a movie: Young lady marries street racer; becomes street racer; builds real race car and overcomes male prejudice and personal tragedies to break down gender barriers, dominate racing, and win championships.

The former Shirley Roque was just a teenager when she married Jack Muldowney. Their love of speed carried Shirley first into gas dragsters in the 1960s and then, with the aid of mentor Connie Kalitta, into the volatile world of Funny Cars. Muldowney, divorced from her husband, earned her Funny Car license in 1971 and won the IHRA Southern Invitational later that year.

After suffering severe burns in a Funny Car fire, Muldowney switched to Top Fuel in 1975 and, with the help of Kalitta, now her boyfriend, set the world on fire in another way. She became the first woman to contest an NHRA final round at the 1975 Springnationals, where she lost to Marvin Graham, and later in the year was runner-up at the US Nationals to Don Garlits, who would be her arch-rival years later.

Muldowney only had to wait a year to win her first race, at the 1976 Springnationals, where she beat Bob Edwards for the first of 18 career victories. Muldowney got better in 1977 and won her first of three NHRA championships. More championships followed, in 1980 and 1982 on the NHRA circuit, and in 1981 on the AHRA tour. Her 1982 campaign was capped with an emotional U.S. Nationals win, which culminated with a final-round victory over her now-estranged boyfriend Kalitta.

Hollywood thought it sounded good, too, and in 1983 released 'Heart Like A Wheel,' which chronicled her amazing story, but there was more.

Muldowney's world was shattered in June 1984, when she lost a front tire at 247 mph at NHRA's Grandnational in Quebec and crashed heavily. She overcame crippling leg injuries and returned to racing in 1986, but her comeback was fraught with problems. Though she continued to finish in the Top 10 points standings and became a member of the exclusive 4-Second Club, her victory at the 1989 Fallnationals, her first since the accident, was also her last.

The high expense of racing forced Muldowney to the sidelines temporarily, and off the NHRA circuit permanently in the early 1990s, though she continued to draw large crowds for match-race dates and her appearances on the IHRA circuit.

PRUDHOMME

Few drag racing nicknames are appropriate as 'the Snake' moniker bestowed upon rail-thin Don Prudhomme at an early age. In a driving career that spanned 29 years, Prudhomme's deadly strikes made him just as feared as the cobra logo that adorned his cars.

Prudhomme was just 20 when he burst into the limelight with a victory at the prestigious March Meet at the wheel of the Zeuschel-Fuller-Prudhomme entry. That led to Prudhomme's tenure in the nearly unbeatable Greer-Black-Prudhomme dragster and finally behind the wheel of 'The Hawaiian' of legendary car owner Roland Leong.

It was there that Prudhomme began cutting a swath through NHRA competition. He won the 1965 Winternationals and US Nationals, becoming the first to win both in a single season, then won the Nationals again in 1969 and 1970. Prudhomme switched to Funny Car in 1972 and resumed his winning ways, winning Indy again in 1973 and 1974.

He won his first of four straight NHRA championships in 1975, capturing six of the eight events, and capped the year with the sport's first five second and 240 mph passes at the NHRA Supernationals. Incredibly, he bettered that record in 1976, winning seven of eight en route to his second championship and, in 1982, became the first Funny Car driver to exceed 250 mph. Despite relinquishing his title in 1979, Prudhomme still placed in the top ten every year (finishing second three times) except 1986, which he sat out while wooing the US Tobacco Company to sponsor him through its Skoal brand. The company remained with him through his tough transition back to Top Fuel in 1990 and until his retirement in 1994.

Prudhomme finished a dismal 13th in his return to dragsters, then rode three wins and four runner-ups to a third-place finish in 1991, where he also joined the four Second Club, and three wins in 1992 placed him sixth. Despite becoming the third member of the 300-mph club, his 1993 season was a disaster with no wins and a career-worst finish of 14th. He bounced back for his 'Final Strike' tour in 1994 and went out in style, winning three races and finishing second in points.

Prudhomme won NHRA national-event titles in four decades and finished with 49 wins—35 in Funny Car and 14 in Top Fuel—then settled into the role of car owner for protégés Larry Dixon in Top Fuel and Ron Capps in Funny Car.

SHEPHERD

With a tousle of red hair and boyish looks, Lee Shepherd hardly looked like a championship race car driver when he entered the ranks of NHRA Pro Stock competition in 1976 at age 32. It only took one look into a pair of gunfighter eyes to know that he was serious—deadly serious—about winning.

Shepherd cut his racing teeth as a bracket racer in the late 1960s, then moved into NHRA's competitive Modified Production class in 1972. Two years later, he joined forces with Texas engine builders David Reher and Buddy Morrison to form the vaunted Reher-Morrison-Shepherd triumvirate that would dominate racing in the 1980s.

The team won the 1974 Winternationals, the first of 30 titles for the soft-spoken Fort Worth, Texas, native. In 1976, they graduated to the Pro Stock class and won the Cajun Nationals, but Shepherd rolled the team's Camaro later that year at the Summernationals and hung up his Pro Stock driving shoes for more than a year, during which time he returned to Modified and won the 1977 Cajun Nationals.

In 1978, the trio reformed and Shepherd and the R-M-S Camaro won the Division 4 title. After a similar success in 1979, the team catapulted to the top of the Pro Stock ranks in 1980, winning the season-opening Winternationals and five more titles. He entered the season-ending Winston World Finals with the points lead, but lost the World Championship to Bob Glidden when his transmission broke in the second round.

That was the last time until his death that someone other than Shepherd would win the NHRA title. He won four straight NHRA championships from 1981 through 1984 and racked up an incredible 158-29 record while winning. In 1982, where he went 35-6, he was in the final round of 11 of the 12 events.

Shepherd's glorious career came to a sudden and tragic ending March 11, 1985, during a test session when his Camaro inexplicably got airborne and tumbled, ejecting Shepherd from the car, killing him instantly.

THE CARS

Joe Amato Top Fueler (1984)

Joe Amato's Keystone Auto Parts Top Fueler may not have changed the shape of Top Fuel in 1984 like Don Garlits' first rear-engined dragster in 1971, but it certainly did change its profile.

When Amato's Al Swindahl-built dragster was rolled out of its trailer for the Gatornationals in mid-March 1984, many of his fellow fuel racers rolled their eyes and laughed at the car's enormously high rear stabilizer wing, propped atop obscenely long struts nearly twice the height of every other car on the grounds.

Before the event concluded, Amato's adversaries were rolling their eyes for a different reason, and the only people laughing were Amato and all of the nation's chassis builders, who were soon filling orders for tall wings.

Designed by Indy car guru Eldon Rasmussen, the tall wing took advantage of a very simple principle: leverage. But placing the wing high and behind the rear wheels, crew chief Tim Richards could apply more downforce to the rear tires to keep them planted without running

more 'angle of attack' in the wing, which would create horsepower-robbing aerodynamic drag. According to Rasmussen, the new-design wing freed up as much as 300 horsepower.

Rasmussen's design allowed Richards to have the best of both worlds, and it only took one run to prove it. On its maiden voyage, the car ran 257.87 mph, tying the fastest run in history. Amato duplicated that speed twice more before upping it to 259.36, then shattered the 260-mph barrier with a run of 260.11 in the

semifinals. Incredibly, Amato improved on that speed with an astounding blast of 262.39 mph in the final round.

The car eventually ran as fast as 264.70 mph (his 1983 car's best was 254 mph!), and he ran four straight 260 mph speeds en route to winning the NorthStar Nationals. The revolutionary car carried Amato to his first of a record-breaking five Winston championships that year and defined the new profile of the class with a design that is still mandatory for winning in the 1990s.

Kenny Bernstein Tempo Funny Car (1984)

The victories claimed by Kenny Bernstein's 1984 Budweiser King Ford Tempo Funny Car don't show up in the NHRA record books; they show up on every car competing in the class today.

Bernstein and longtime crew chief Dale Armstrong always have been innovators, but when they teamed with Ford engineers in late 1983 at the Lockheed wind tunnel in Georgia for two days of aerodynamic experimentation on their Tempo body, the die was cast for a new generation of racer.

Major modifications to the body included lips on the leading edge of the front spoiler to force the air into the grille, where it would be deflected over the car's roof, wraparound fender skirts and fully enclosed side windows to keep air rushing by the side of the car from getting inside the body and creating drag; a rear belly pan to avoid a high-pressure area under the car's tail; and a taller rear-deck spoiler to keep the rear end planted.

The car registered a whopping 420 pounds less aerodynamic drag (940 versus 1360) than their previous Mercury LN-7 and ten percent better than the previous year's box-stock Tempo body. The car's aerodynamic prowess became clear just two months after the car debuted as Bernstein guided the trick-laden Tempo to the class' first 260-mph pass, in the final round of the Gatornationals, the only race the car won. As other Funny Car teams embraced the aero technology, the mile-per-hour barriers fell quickly:

Bernstein broke 270 two years later with a third-generation wind-tunnel Tempo and Mike Dunn ran 280 in 1987. Six years later, Jim Epler topped 300 mph in a car not very different in theory from the Bud King Tempo.

The 1984 Bud King also sported a revolutionary data logger that recorded 32 channels of information; once the worth of that data became known to his competitors, they also jumped on that bandwagon, and today no car runs without one.

Cook & Bedwell Top Eliminator dragster (1957)

On a fateful February day in 1957, the face of drag racing changed dramatically. On that beautiful California day, at the legendary quarter-mile known as Lion's Drag Strip in Wilmington, just south of Los Angeles, Emery Cook wheeled his and Cliff Bedwell's Top Eliminator dragster to an unheard-of speed of 166.97 mph, a full seven miles per hour faster than the previous acknowledged best. Cook's runs were so unbelievable that the strip's operators invited everyone to verify the numbers and then laboratory-tested the clocks the next day for accuracy.

The magic behind Cook's amazing run was in the fuel tank, where a mix of nitromethane percolated and fed the ravenous Bruce Crower-tuned 354-inch carbureted Chrysler Hemi. The car, built by the day's acknowledged master, Scotty Fenn, measured a short 100 inches.

Two months later, Cook recorded the first eight-second pass in drag racing history, an 8.89 at Bakersfield in central California, and, a few weeks later, upped his speed mark to 168 mph.

Before long, the hue and cry from Cook's competitors—concerned about escalating costs and the parts attrition caused by the treacheries of running the sometimes explosive and often tempestuous firewater known as nitro—and track operators, concerned about safety and stopping distances on tracks built for slower speeds, led to a temporary ban on the use of nitromethane by NHRA at many, but not all, top tracks. Never before had one vehicle caused such a stir and affected the rulebook.

Cook continued to run fuel at the tracks that allowed nitromethane, and with the sanctioning bodies, such as the American Hot Rod Association, who also saw the future of the sport as being nitro-fueled. Cook's car, which won most of the races it entered, finished the season with a huge Top Eliminator win at the AHRA Nationals in Great Bend, Kansas.

Every modern-day 300-inch wheelbase, 320-mph Top Fueler owes its lineage to the 100-inch wheelbased marvel called the Cook & Bedwell dragster.

John Force Castrol GTX Pontiac Funny Car (1996)

Corporate sponsorships and widely available technology have brought incredible parity to drag racing competition in the 1990s, which makes John Force's 1996 Winston championship-winning Firebird Funny Car all the more special.

Entering the 1996 season, Force sought to break two significant ties he held with other racers. The first, five Winston championships, was shared with multitime Top Fuel champ Joe Amato. The second was his record of 11 event victories in a season, which he had accomplished in 1993 to match Pro Stock racer Darrell Alderman's 1991 record.

Considering that Force's 1995 campaign had yielded just six victories, after posting ten wins in 1994 and the aforementioned 11 in 1993, experts figured that the class finally had caught up to Force, who had captured season titles in 1990, 1992, 1993, 1994, and 1995. In 1995, archrivals Al Hofmann and Cruz Pedregon each had captured five wins and figured to give Force a three-horse race in 1996. It didn't happen that way.

After losing the final round of the season-opening Winternationals to Hofmann, Force won 13 of the remaining 18 events en route to breaking his ties with Amato and Alderman. Force's green and white Pontiac, tuned by Austin Coil and Bernie Fedderly, qualified No. 1 at 13 national events and recorded low elapsed time at 14 events. At four events, Force swept all honors by qualifying No. 1, and recording low elapsed time and top speed. He also recorded four of the five quickest Funny Car times in NHRA history, including the top three while racking up his 91 percent win ratio with a record of 65 wins and only six losses, three of which came in final rounds.

Force won his record sixth Winston championship by a landslide 636 points over his own teammate, Tony Pedregon, who fielded a second, near-identical Castrol Pontiac, ostensibly as a research and development mule for the number-one car, but Pedregon turned it into a winner—he beat Force in the final round of the Fram Nationals—and finished second only to his boss.

AND THE WINNER IS... *The 1996 season looked like being a three-horse race but John Force changed all that.*

Don Garlits' 'Wynn's Charger' Top Fueler (1971)

There had been other rear-engined dragsters before Don Garlits debuted his Swamp Rat 14 in 1971, but the few that had been successful were powered by gasoline-burning engines. Front-engined '"slingshots'—so-named because the driver sat behind the rear wheels like a rock in a slingshot—ruled Top Fuel in the late 1960s and no 'middie,' as the rear-engined cars were perhaps more correctly called, could come within a half-second of the top slingshots—if they could stay off the guardrails at all.

Don Garlits' own front-engined Wynn's Charger, Swamp Rat 13, was itself unstoppable until March 8, 1970, when the transmission, nestled between his legs, exploded as he hammered the throttle in the final round of the AHRA Grand American race against Richard Tharp at Lions Drag Strip in Southern California just a week after winning the NHRA Gatornationals in his homestate of Florida. The explosion severed half of Garlits' right foot and broke his left leg and foot, but did not sever his appetite for racing or innovation.

As Garlits sat convalescing in Pacific Coast Hospital in Long Beach, California, he drew up plans for a rear-engined machine that, once the kinks were worked out, would prove the prototype for Top Fuel's future. Once Garlits figured out how to handle the car's darty steering by slowing the steering ratio, the car resumed its predecessor's winning ways.

Garlits returned to racing in 1971 and won the AHRA World championship and four other AHRA events, the NHRA Winternationals and Springnationals, and the tradi-tion-rich March Meet with the radical new car, and owned both AHRA and NHRA national records. Garlits almost exactly duplicated those feats the following year, winning ten national events in NHRA, AHRA, and IHRA competition, and again won the AHRA championship. Garlits' opponents were slow to make the change, but by 1973, once racers realized the performance and safety benefits—they were, after all, now sitting in front of a perpetually oil-slinging, fire-emitting, nitro-burning beast—the slingshot had been relegated to history.

Greer-Black-Prudhomme Top Fueler (1962)

In 1962, Don Prudhomme was a respected up-and-coming driver, but not yet 'the Snake' in terms of reputation. The fabled Greer-Black-Prudhomme Top Fuel dragster made him famous, and so did the wild claims of a perhaps overzealous advertising copy writer. In a 1964 advertisement in Drag News, then the sport's Bible, the Scheifer clutch company claimed that the G-B-P dragster—running one of its clutches, of course—had compiled an unbelievable 236-7 win-loss record from mid-1962 through 1964.

Historians over time may finally have discounted those claims—drag racing expert Chris Martin, author of The Top Fuel Handbook, painstakingly went through old race reports to arrive at a more accurate (and believable!) record of 81-8—but the car's performances and winning record still are incredible considering the vast number of Top Fuel cars then and the talent level of the drivers and mechanics in the hotbed of fuel racing.

With Prudhomme at the wheel, the legendary engine builder Keith Black on wrenches, and machinist non parallel Tom Greer providing the wallet, the Greer-Black-Prudhomme dragster dominated Southern California Top Fuel action, especially at Lions Drag Strip, where Prudhomme won seven straight times from June 17, 1962, before red-lighting to 'T.V. Tommy' Ivo in late September. Prudhomme seldom failed to make the final round and almost always won, and extended his mastery to the other Southern California tracks like San Gabriel and Pomona. The G-B-P car set track records, top speeds, and low elapsed times nearly everywhere it went.

The car itself, which was restored and presented to Prudhomme when he retired from driving at the end of 1994, was built by Kent Fuller from chromoly tubing (a first) and was built around the components rather than having them added as afterthoughts. The combination of those innovations and Black's ability to tune the clutch and power output to varying track conditions from week to week and surface to surface made this car all but unbeatable.

Bill Jenkins' 'Grumpy's Toy' Vega Pro Stocker (1972)

In the early 1970s, Chrysler-powered cars ruled Pro Stock, which, one could say, made one Chevy stalwart a little grumpy. Bill 'Grumpy' Jenkins had opened the decade by winning the first two races of the inaugural Pro Stock season in 1970, the Winternationals in California and the Gatornationals in Florida, but every race for the next two years save one—the 1971 Summernationals, won by Don Nicholson in a Ford Maverick—were won by Chrysler Hemi-powered cars, and

Mopar star Ronnie Sox captured World Championship titles in both 1970 and 1971.

Jenkins was determined to change that. When he rolled into the Pomona Raceway pits for the 1972 Winternationals, inside his trailer was a new 'Grumpy's Toy' Pro Stocker that would forever change the class: a radical small-block Chevrolet-powered Vega built by SRD (Speed Research & Development), a project that was inspired by NHRA's new rules for 1972 that gave lighter weight breaks

to small-block wedge engines. After qualifying 17th in the 32-car field with a disappointing 9.90, he stepped up his performance to a string of 9.60s on Sunday. He defeated No. 1 qualifier Stu McDade in the first round and went on to defeat four more Mopar Hemis on his way to the win, knocking out Don Grotheer in the final.

But for a steering wheel malfunction at the Gatornationals and his failure to attend the US Nationals in 1972 (in deference to running Don Garlits' anti-NHRA PRO event in

Tulsa the same weekend as a show of support), Jenkins was undefeated in NHRA national event competition, earning a then-incredible $250,000 for the season in purse winnings, sponsorship support, and contingencies.

For his accomplishments, Jenkins was the first NHRA racer to be featured in Time Magazine, and he continued to be a dominant factor in Pro Stock during the 1970s, an era highlighted by his 1976 Winston championship season with Larry Lombardo as the driver.

Larry Minor Top Fueler (1983)

Rarely in the modern era of Top Fuel racing has a single car dominated the performance standards as the Gary Beck-driven, Larry Minor-owned Top Fueler did in 1983. Minor, a wealthy Southern California potato farmer, and Beck, a veteran Top Fuel driver who first made his mark on the sport with a stunning debut victory at the 1972 US Nationals, ruled Top Fuel and won the Winston championship in 1983 by sheer brute force.

Their blue machine, constructed under the watchful eye of Top Fuel's 1980s guru, Al Swindahl, already had established itself as the quickest on the planet when it recorded a 5.484, the first 5.4-second clocking in history, at the 1982 US Nationals. Breaking that barrier was not new to Beck, who also had steered Minor's other lookalike cars to the first 5.6- and first 5.5-second runs in history, but even he couldn't have been ready for the assault on the timers that he launched in 1983.

Over the course of the 1983 season, the Beck/Minor machine, tuned by Bernie Fedderly, who would go on to future glory as crew chief Austin Coil's right-hand-man on John Force's all-conquering Funny Cars, recorded 16 of the 17 quickest elapsed times in history—from their barrier-breaking 5.391 clocking at the Golden Gate Nationals in Northern California to the 5.51 Beck ran at the season-ending Winston Finals in Southern California—moving the 5.48, so amazing a run a year earlier, down to eleventh quickest.

The 5.39, Beck's fourth straight barrier-breaker, came in the final round of the Golden Gates, where Beck laid away Gary Ormsby for his fourth win of the season, tying the record then held by Shirley Muldowney, Don Garlits, and Kelly Brown. Beck, who also won the Gatornationals, Southern Nationals, and US Nationals, duplicated that 5.391 number a week later at the Winston Finals, where he also ran the fourth quickest pass, 5.434.

Don Nicholson's 'Eliminator I' Comet Funny Car (1966)

If the Cook & Bedwell Top Eliminator dragster is one of the fathers of Top Fuel, then so could it be argued that 'Dyno Don' Nicholson's 'Eliminator I' '66 Comet helped in the birth of the modern-day Funny Car. Although the Funny Car class' lineage stretches back into the Super Stock, Experimental Stock, and Factory Experimental classes, Nicholson's Comet was one of the first tube-framed cars with a removable fiberglass-replica body, a trend that still exists 30 years later.

Lincoln/Mercury's Al Turner designed the machine, specifying chassis layout and suspension and rigidity factors, and had the famed Logghe Bros. chassis shop built five of the machines, topping each with a body straight from factory molds. Originally designed as a one-piece body that would be completely lifted off the car for better access to the engine and driver's compartment, the Logghes later figured that the body need only be hinged at the rear, creating a flip-top body that led to the sobriquet 'flopper.'

Nicholson, Jack Chrisman, and 'Fast Eddie' Schartman all received one of the cars, but Nicholson's car was nearly unbeatable, often outperforming his opponents by a full quarter-second and winning 29 straight races. Nicholson's Comet even clocked a still-controversial 7.96, the first seven-second pass for a bodied car.

The Comets dominated the Experimental Stock class for a full two years, but as speeds increased, these first Funny Cars which were aerodynamically crude by today's standards, tried to get airborne. Nicholson's Comet eventually made its last run during a test session at Irwindale Raceway in California. The body flexed under high speeds and the latches failed, sending the body off the chassis and practically into orbit. Despite what are seen as its aerodynamic flaws, Turner directed the onsite engineers to burn what remained of the body so that no one could copy its technology.

Don Prudhomme's US Army Monza Funny Car (1975-76)

Five years after he built his first Funny Car, former Top Fuel ace Don Prudhomme ruled his new class with an iron fist for the next four. No car was more feared than 'the Snake's' 1975 Chevy Monza, and his sponsorship from the US Army was very appropriate. The mighty Monza was as unstoppable as a tank and delivered winning runs with deadly consistency and the impact of an artillery shell.

In 1975, Prudhomme and crew chief Bob Brandt won six of NHRA's eight races and won the Winston championship, his first, by a whopping 5,500-point margin. In the course, Prudhomme's super Chevy also became the first Funny Car to record a five-second elapsed time, a 5.98, and the first 240-mph pass, a 241.25, at the 1975 Supernationals at Ontario Motor Speedway, then the quickest quarter-mile in the world. He lost only in the first round of the Summernationals, to lifelong rival Tom McEwen, and in the final round of the U.S. Nationals to Raymond Beadle, who would win three straight championships after Prudhomme's reign ended.

As impossible as it may seem, Prudhomme and his Monza outdid themselves the following year by winning seven of the eight races, losing only to Gary Burgin in the final round of the race he wanted to win most, the prestigious US Nationals. Prudhomme finished with a 31-1 record and a 6,100-point edge over second-place finisher Shirl Greer.

Prudhomme's performance advantage was very noticeable on the scoreboards; he had low e.t. or was the No. 1 qualifier at 11 of those 16 events. Years later, Prudhomme finally acknowledged that the source of his victories was not merely superior horsepower, but, as Keith Black had taught him years ago with the also nearly invincible Greer-Black-Prudhomme Top Fueler, the ability to successfully transfer that power to the ground through the clutch. It was a knowledge that served him well through two more Winston championships in the subsequent years.

AWARDS

NHRA Winston Rookie of the Year

TIME AND A HALF *K.C. Spurlock won the 1990 award and $10,000. Since 1993 however the award has been raised to $20,000.*

Each year since 1990, the RJ Reynolds Company, which sponsors the NHRA Winston Drag Racing Series of 23 national events through its Winston cigarette brand, also sponsors the association's Rookie of the Year award.

Funny Car driver K.C. Spurlock was the first recipient of the award and received the $10,000 cash award for his sixth-place finish that season. Funny Car racer Del Worsham won in 1991, also with a sixth-place finish, and teenage Top Fuel racer Dannielle DePorter, who finished tenth in the Winston standings, took top honors in 1993.

In 1993, the cash award was raised to $20,000, and Pro Stock standout Kurt Johnson, son of former Winston champ Warren Johnson, was honored after an incredible second-place finish behind his father. In 1994, Top Fuel racer Bob Vandergriff Jr. was judged the best newcomer, followed the next year by another Top Fuel sensation, Larry Dixon Jr., who won three events in his rookie season and finished third in the points standings.

For the first time in the award's history, Rookie of the Year honors were split in 1996 between Pro Stock competitor Mike Edwards and Pro Stock Bike racer Matt Hines. Edwards, a former Winston champion in the Modified class, finished third in his first full year in the ultra-competitive Pro Stock class while Hines, son of two-wheeled legend Byron Hines, finished third in the motorcycle class despite never having ridden competitively. Each received a $10,000 check

Don Prudhomme Award

HOW TO GET A HEAD *Don Prudhomme with his namesake award created in 1994.*

The Don Prudhomme award, created by NHRA in October 1994 in honor of legendary driver Prudhomme, who retired from racing at the end of that year, is given annually by NHRA to an individual who has made a profound impact on the growth and positive image of NHRA Winston Drag Racing.

NHRA founder and board chairman Wally Parks, whose vision and guidance helped make NHRA drag racing what is is today, was a natural first winner of the award and had his name affixed to the perpetual crystal trophy.

T. Wayne Robertson, Parks' counterpart with longtime NHRA sponsor and partner R.J. Reynolds'

Sports Marketing arm, was the surprise recipient in the award's second year. It has been Robertson's belief in the value of NHRA drag racing that led to innovation programs such as the Winston Top 10 program that pushed the company's cash contributions to in excess of $2 million annually.

The 1996 winner was honored

posthumously. Leslie Lovett, photo editor of the NHRA and its weekly publication, National DRAGSTER, had covered and exposed the sport of drag racing for more than 30 years before he died of a heart attack in July 1996. His death saddened fans and competitors worldwide who treasured his photography and friendly presence at the track.

Blaine Johnson Award

The newest award presented by the NHRA, the Blaine Johnson Award, was born of great tragedy in 1996. Blaine Johnson, a popular Top Fuel driver and four time Winston Alcohol Dragster champion, died from injuries suffered in a qualifying accident

at the 1996 US Nationals, and the award honors his memory.

Johnson and his older brother and crew chief, Alan, had worked hard from simple beginnings, raised on the family farm with the ethic that hard work would produce its own rewards, and it was true. The brothers worked

hard to learn what it took to win, then used it to its fullest until they became practically unbeatable in Alcohol Dragster. Blaine was leading the Top Fuel points race in just their second full season when he was killed as the result of an engine failure that sent the car out of control.

The award is presented to the individual who shows perseverance and dedication to NHRA Winston Drag Racing. It was only fitting then that the first winner was Alan Johnson, who shared his brother's dream and helped him attain it.

Road to the Future Award

BACKING A WINNER *Tony Pedregon looking forward to a bright future after a very good start.*

The Automobile Club of Southern California Road to the Future Award, presented for the first time in 1996, will be given annually to the NHRA competitor who appears destined for future greatness. The 1996 recipient, Tony Pedregon, truly embodied that statement.

The son of legendary racer 'Flaming Frank' Pedregon and younger brother of 1992 Winston Funny Car champ Cruz Pedregon, Tony got his big chance in 1996 in the number-two Castrol GTX machine of Funny Car champ John Force. He made it the number-two car in more ways than one.

Pedregon, 31, won one race, appeared in seven final rounds and finished second in the NHRA Winston point standings in his first full season in a Funny Car. Pedregon also included qualifying No. 1 twice, becoming the second-quickest Funny Car driver in NHRA history and the fifth member of the Castrol 4-Second Club for Funny Cars.

NHRA Manufacturers Cup

The automobile manufacturer whose current-year models earn the most points for qualifying and category victories at NHRA Winston Drag Racing Series national and divisional events is awarded the NHRA Manufacturers Cup for performance achievement at the season's end.

Points are awarded to entries in Pro Stock, Super Stock and Stock as follows: 60 points for an eliminator victory, 40 points for an eliminator runner-up and 20 points for an eliminator qualification.

Pontiac earned its first NHRA Manufacturers Cup in 1996 partially as a result of the efforts by Jim Yates, who became the first Pontiac driver to win an NHRA Winston Pro Stock championship in his McDonald's Pontiac Firebird, and Peter Biondo, who won the NHRA Winston Super Stock championship in the Hatari Racing Pontiac Firebird.

Since Ford won the first of its three Cups, in 1964, the program's first year, all of the Big Three have won. Chevrolet won 14 cups, dominating the 1970s and early 1980s for General Motors before Oldsmobile set a record in 1995 for most consecutive wins, 12, from 1984-1995. Plymouth has one victory that it gained in 1970.

STATISTICS

BEST WINNING RECORDS, THROUGH 1996

1.	225-50	(.818)	John Myers, Birmingham, Ala., Pro Stock Motorcycle
2.	266-61	(.814)	Dave Schultz, Fort Myers, Fla., Pro Stock Motorcycle
3.	788-221	(.781)	Bob Glidden, Whiteland, Ind., Pro Stock
4.	187-59	(.756)	Darrell Alderman, Morehead, Ky., Pro Stock
5.	486-176	(.735)	John Force, Yorba Linda, Calif., Funny Car
6.	546-205	(.727)	Warren Johnson, Duluth, Ga., Pro Stock
7.	173-85	(.671)	Cruz Pedregon, Camarillo, Calif., Top Fuel, Funny Car
8.	389-194	(.667)	Joe Amato, Old Forge, Pa., Top Fuel
9.	418-213	(.664)	Kenny Bernstein, Dallas, Funny Car, Top Fuel
10.	139-74	(.653)	Scott Geoffrion, Aliso Viejo, Calif., Pro Stock
11.	109-64	(.631)	Kurt Johnson, Lawrenceville, Ga., Pro Stock
12.	141-85	(.624)	Jim Yates, Alexandria, Va., Pro Stock
13.	144-90	(.615)	Cory McClenathan, Anaheim, Calif., Top Fuel
14.	150-97	(.607)	Scott Kalitta, Chelsea, Mich., Funny Car, Top Fuel
15.	183-119	(.606)	Al Hofmann, Umatilla, Fla., Funny Car
16.	153-100	(.605)	Chuck Etchells, Putnam, Conn., Funny Car
	280-183	(.605)	Mark Oswald, Houma, La, Top Fuel, Funny Car
18.	73-54	(.574)	John Smith, Minneapolis, Pro Stock Motorcycle
19.	188-140	(.573)	Mike Dunn, Mount Joy, Pa., Funny Car, Top Fuel
20.	193-149	(.564)	Bruce Allen, Arlington, Texas, Pro Stock
21.	208-164	(.559)	Eddie Hill, Wichita Falls, Texas, Top Fuel
22.	171-136	(.557)	Larry Morgan, Newark, Ohio, Pro Stock
23.	100-82	(.549)	John Mafaro, Saddlebrook, N.J., Pro Stock Motorcycle
24.	38-32	(.542)	Tony Pedregon, Gardena, Calif., Funny Car
25.	79-78	(.503)	Steve Schmidt, Indianapolis, Pro Stock
	81-79	(.503)	Del Worsham, Orange, Calif., Funny Car, Top Fuel

TOP FIVE IN NHRA PROFESSIONAL CAREER VICTORIES, THROUGH 1996:

TOP FUEL:

Joe Amato, Old Forge, Pa.	36
Don Garlits, Ocala, Fla.	35
Gary Beck, Laguna Nigel, Calif.	19
Shirley Muldowney, Armada, Mich.	18
Darrell Gwynn, Miami	18

FUNNY CAR:

John Force, Yorba Linda, Calif.	61
Don Prudhomme, Granada Hills, Calif.	35
Kenny Bernstein, Dallas	30
Ed McCulloch, Hemet, Calif.	18
Mark Oswald, Houma, La	18

JOE AMATO *Who has been having success after success in the Top Fuelers.*

PRO STOCK:

Bob Glidden, Whiteland, Ind.	85
Warren Johnson, Duluth, Ga.	59
Lee Shepherd, Arlington, Texas	26
Darrell Alderman, Morehead, Ky.	23
Bruce Allen, Arlington, Texas	12

PRO STOCK MOTORCYCLE:

Dave Schultz, Fort Myers, Fla.	41
John Myers, Birmingham, Ala.	30
Terry Vance, Santa Fe Springs, Calif.	24
John Mafaro, Saddlebrook, N.J.	6
Bob Carpenter, Wayne, N.J.	3

PAT AUSTIN *in his Top Alcohol Funny Car.*

TOP NHRA NATIONAL EVENT SEASON ROUND WINS:

John Force, Yorba Linda, Calif., Funny Car	(1996)	65*
Darrell Alderman, Morehead, Ky., Pro Stock	(1991)	59
Force, Funny Car	(1993)	57
Bob Glidden, Whiteland, Ind., Pro Stock	(1989)	52*
Warren Johnson, Sugar Hill, Ga., Pro Stock	(1993)	52
Force, Funny Car	(1994)	50
Force, Funny Car	(1995)	50*
Bruce Larson, Dauphin, Pa., Funny Car	(1989)	48*
Force, Funny Car	(1991)	48
Johnson, Pro Stock	(1992)	48
Darrell Alderman, Pro Stock	(1994)	48
Johnson, Pro Stock	(1995)	48*
Joe Amato, Old Forge, Pa.	(1990)	47*
Gary Ormsby, Roseville, Calif., Top Fuel	(1990)	47*

*Indicates 19 events

LEADERS IN NHRA NATIONAL EVENT VICTORIES (ALL CATEGORIES, THROUGH 1996):

1.	Bob Glidden, Whiteland, Ind., Pro Stock	85
2	Pat Austin, Tacoma, Wash., Top Alcohol Funny Car (57)/Top Fuel (5)	62
3.	John Force, Yorba Linda, Calif., Funny Car	61
4.	Warren Johnson, Duluth, Ga., Pro Stock	59
5.	*Don Prudhomme, Granada Hills, Calif., Top Fuel (14)/Funny Car (35)	49
6.	Kenny Bernstein, Dallas, Funny Car (30)/Top Fuel (16)	46
7.	Joe Amato, Old Forge, Pa., Pro Comp (5)/Top Fuel (36)	41
	Dave Schultz, Fort Myers, Fla., Pro Stock Motorcycle	41
9.	*Don Garlits, Ocala, Fla., Top Fuel	35
10.	*Blaine Johnson, Santa Maria, Calif., Top Alcohol Dragster (26)/Top Fuel (4)	30
	John Myers, Birmingham, Ala., Pro Stock Motorcycle	30
12.	*Lee Shepherd, Arlington, Texas, Modified/Pro Stock	29
	David Nickens, Houston, Competition	29
14.	*Darrell Gwynn, Miami, Top Alcohol Dragster (10)/Top Fuel (18)	28
15.	Bob Newberry, Schenectady, N.Y., Competition/Top Alcohol Funny Car	27
16.	Darrell Alderman, Morehead, Ky., Pro Stock	26
17.	Edmond Richardson, Goodlettsville, Tenn., Super Comp/Super Street	25
18.	*Brad Anderson, LaVerne, Calif., Top Alcohol Funny Car	24
	*Terry Vance, Santa Fe Springs, Calif., Fuel Motorcycle/Pro Stock Motorcycle	24
20.	Bill Barney, Knoxville, Tenn., Top Alcohol Dragster	23
	Scotty Richardson, Goodlettsville, Tenn., Super Gas/Super Comp/Stock	23

22.	*Ed McCulloch, Hemet, Calif., Funny Car (18)/Top Fuel (4)	22
	Frank Manzo, Morganville, N.J., Top Alcohol Funny Car	22
24.	Cruz Pedregon, Camarillo, Calif., TAD/TAFC (4)/Funny Car (17)	21
	Jeff Taylor, Lumberton, N.C., Stock/Super Stock/Super Comp	21
26.	Mark Oswald, Houma, La., Top Fuel (2)/Funny Car (18)	20
27.	*Gary Beck, Laguna Niguel, Calif., Top Fuel	19
28.	*Shirley Muldowney, Mount Clemens, Mich., Top Fuel	18
	Tom Conway, Seminole, Okla., Top Alcohol Dragster	18
30.	*Dave Boertman, Fruitport, Mich., Stock/Super Stock	17
31.	Mike Dunn, Mount Joy, Pa., Funny Car (10)/Top Fuel (6)	16
	Tony Bartone, Manhasset, N.Y., Top Alcohol Funny Car	16
33.	*Dick LaHaie, Lansing, Mich., Top Fuel	15
	Larry Morgan, Newark, Ohio, Super Stock/Comp (7)/Pro Stock (8)	15
	Vern Moats, Des Moines, Iowa, Top Alcohol Funny Car	15
	*Ronnie Sox, Burlington, N.C., Super Stock (6)/Pro Stock (9)	15
	David Rampy, Woodland, Ala., Super Gas/Super Stock/Comp/Super Comp	15
38.	*Gary Ormsby, Roseville, Calif., Top Fuel	14
	Scott Kalitta, Chelsea, Mich., Funny Car (1)/Top Fuel (13)	14
40.	Bruce Allen, Arlington, Texas, Modified (1)/Pro Stock (12)	13
	Bobby Warren, Clinton, N.C., Stock/Super Stock	13
	*Bill Jenkins, Malvern, Pa., Super Stock/Pro Stock	13
	*Raymond Beadle, Dallas, Texas, Funny Car	13
	*Ken Veney, Wadsworth, Ohio, Top Alcohol Dragster/Top Alcohol Funny Car	13
	Larry Kopp, Baltimore, Modified/Competition	13
	Eddie Hill, Wichita Falls, Texas, Top Fuel	13
	Randy Anderson, Ontario, Calif., Top Alcohol Funny Car	13
48.	John Lingenfelter, Decatur, Ind., Super Stock/Comp	12
	Al Hofmann, Umatilla, Fla., Funny Car	12
	*Dale Armstrong, Torrance, Calif., Pro Comp	12
	*Bill Walsh, Scranton, Pa., Top Alcohol Dragster	12
	*Billy Meyer, Waco, Texas, Funny Car	12
	Jay Payne, Upland, Calif., Top Alcohol Dragster	12
	Bobby Taylor, Laguna Hills, Calif., Top Alcohol Dragster	12

*indicates no longer active driver in NHRA national events

RAYMOND BEADLE *and his 1981 Winston winning Funny Car, Blue Max.*

OFF-ROAD MOTOR SPORTS

Off-road motorsports, or 'off-roading', as it has become generally known, offers a variety of challenge, quite different from any other motorsport. It draws out our adventurous nature, much like the explorers of old, who set sail in their galleons, in search of what lay across vast expanses of water.

These modern day adventurers, however, sail oceans of dirt, sand, and rock, and their ships are made by Ford, Chevrolet, Dodge, or Toyota. For them, the challenge is to discover what lies around the next corner, or beyond that next mountain rise. It's the sense of discovery and feeling of accomplishment which brings off-roaders out, weekend after weekend, to pit themselves and their vehicles against the most rugged and unforgiving terrain on the planet.

In the Sierra Nevada mountains, jeeps slowly twist and climb their way over the enormous rocks and tight turns of the infamous Rubicon Trail. In the forests and swamps of the east, the mud and inclement weather make trails which challenge even the hardiest trucks and drivers. Within the sandy, rocky confines of the Mojave Desert in the southwest, you can find a plethora of off-road activity. The tube-chassised Sand Rails of the Glamis dunes provide a lightweight, high-horsepower 'E-Ticket' ride in the shifting sands, while Baja Bugs and 4x4s travel down old mining roads, in search of the ghost towns of the old west.

Off-roading has always been a group-oriented sport, whether it's week-long family camping trips in the mountains, or weekends spent watching the races with a few good friends. As the sport has grown, off-roaders have banded together to promote safe and responsible land use, and to better enjoy their preferred activity. Clubs regularly organize events like 'The Easter Jeep Safari' held in Moab, Utah, which bring together hundreds of off-roaders from around the country to experience several days of exploration and excitement in the majestic lands of the American wilderness.

For those of a more competitive nature, race-sanctioning bodies like SCORE, FUD-Race, and the ASDA host some of the most exciting racing events in the world. World-renowned races like the Baja 1000 bring together dozens of corporate sponsors, hundreds of racers, and thousands of fans. For race fans, it's an experience not soon forgotten. For the racers, it's a chance to prove their skill and endurance against the unforgiving desert, and each other. And for the companies, it has become a research and development opportunity, as well as a chance to advertise the fact that their product was tough enough to 'beat the Baja'.

Whether you prefer the recreational or more competitive forms of off-roading, this accessible sport can be enjoyed by nearly everyone. The type of vehicles, variety of terrain, challenges available, and the ways they can be enjoyed are only limited by your imagination!

IN YOUR FACE *Off-roading demands much of driver, machine, and manufacturer, and provides thrills and spills aplenty for the spectator. Which is one of the reasons that it has seen such incredible growth in recent years. As motor sports go, this is definitely one to watch.*

THE HISTORY

The birth of off-road motorsports can be traced back to the very first race between automobiles. Since asphalt as we know it had yet to be invented, it's very likely it was held off-road! In that time, 'off-roading', as it has become known, has steadily evolved into perhaps the most diverse, and certainly one of the most popular, of all American motorsports.

In 1939, the United States Army commissioned the Willys-Overland company to create a viable replacement for the motorcycle sidecars and converted Model-T Fords used during WW1. The result was the original MB 'jeep'.

This four-wheel-drive, 1,200-pound vehicle became an integral part of the US armed forces, playing a multitude of roles under the most extreme conditions. The jeeps' performance prompted Army official Eugene Pyle to say, "It will go places where tanks quit and birds would come back exhausted." Servicemen so loved driving their jeeps off-road they wanted to take them home. Civilian jeeps were quickly put to use, carrying families on many an adventure across the USA.

On the west coast, another product of wartime was making a significant impact on the growing sport of off-roading. The Volkswagen Beetle, or 'Bug', as it became known, made an ideal platform for exploring the deserts of the American Southwest.

Its light weight and rear engine configuration rivaled that of jeeps, giving traction and handling in the deserts' sandy, rocky terrain.

Performance enthusiasts quickly saw its potential, and an entire industry was born to fill the needs created by the Bug's popularity. From the sand dunes of Pismo Beach to the wilds of the Baja California peninsula, VW Bugs were put against every challenge the off-roaders could muster.

As time went on, a 'cross-pollination', of sorts, occurred when each new form of off-roading spread across the country. Advancing technology and innovative enthusiasts continued to advance the sport.

MILITARY INTELLIGENCE *Ex-servicemen in Army-issue jeeps created this peaceful sport.*

Many of today's off-road vehicles are built to perform well in a variety of conditions, and it's not uncommon for an off-roader to enjoy several different forms of off-highway recreation. In garages throughout the country, the family 4x4 often serves double duty as both a trail machine, and a tow vehicle for ATVs, dirt bikes, and the occasional race truck or dune buggy.

Others are built for a specific purpose, abandoning versatility for cutting edge performance on their intended terrain. Vehicles built to take on the deep mud of the east coast are out of their element in the soft, blow-sand conditions of dunes. Likewise, the sand car finds itself ill-equipped to handle a bottomless, loamy, mud bog. When each of these vehicles is in their element, however, the fun comes fast and furious!

Racing vehicles have evolved from their roots as converted automobiles into true racing machines, with technology rivaling that of Indy cars. Today, carbon fiber body panels and tubular chro-moly steel chassis have replaced factory sheet metal and framework. Powertrain spec sheets read like shopping lists of exotic metals and composite alloys. Computer-designed suspensions extract over 36 inches of wheel travel from arcane arrays of springs and levers, enabling controlled speeds of over 140 mph across the open desert.

Around the country, the Bureau of Land Management and the US Forest Service have established Off-Highway Vehicle (OHV) areas, which offer the entire range of off-road challenges. Although they were created to provide OHV access to our public lands and address environmental concerns voiced by various special interest groups, there are many areas of public land open for exploration. For each of these areas, government agencies, together with off-road clubs and organizations, have developed the 'Tread Lightly' program. This common sense set of guidelines underscores the need for careful use of public lands by all outdoor recreationalists.

WIDE RANGE *Off-roading encompasses many disciplines, and motorcycles are a welcome addition to a sport whose major aim is to go anywhere.*

The future of off-road motorsports in the United States—and, in fact, the world—appears to be a bright one. The automotive industry reports that sales of SUVs (Sport Utility Vehicles) are now outpacing automobiles, enabling more people to get involved in off-roading. The Specialty Equipment Manufacturers' Association (SEMA) has seen a consistent increase in off-road equipment makers over the past several years. As if any further proof were needed, off-road clubs and organizations are seeing a steady increase in membership every year.

Off-road racing has seen an increase in both competitors and fan attendance in each of its many forms. New sand and mud racing facilities have been constructed, and filled to capacity at several hot spots around the country, including a world-class sand drag facility in the casino town of Laughlin, Nevada. The trend to host events in places like Laughlin, with its casinos, hotels, and other attractions, is an old idea rediscovered: the SCORE Desert Racing Series held many races in places like Las Vegas in the past, and has decided it's a concept whose time has come again.

Increasing media coverage in print and by television sports channels like ESPN, Prime Sports Network, and others, have further served to bring off-road motorsports into the homes of millions, but perhaps the biggest impact of all has come from the internet. With the click of a mouse, free World Wide Web sites like off-road.com offer up-to-the-minute race results, in-car reporting, vehicle info, 'how to' articles, and more. Enthusiasts, fans, and racers alike have developed their own web sites, featuring everything from their vehicles to favorite terrain. With the internet becoming an integral part of our lives, a large part of off-road's future will be on-line.

THE PETROL-HEAD CONVENTION *Increased media attention has made SCORE and its race events increasingly popular.*

SCORE

Founded by racing legend Mickey Thompson in 1973 as a promotional organization for short course racing in Southern California, SCORE has grown into the world's largest sanctioning body for off-road motorsports. Soon after its inception, Thompson hired *Hot Rod Magazine* editor, Sal Fish, to take the reins as president of the organization, in what would prove to be a milestone event in the history of off-road racing.

Fish created a new race in Parker, Arizona, in 1974, and organized events in Mexicali and San Felipe, Mexico, along with Barstow and Lucerne Valley, California. In 1975, SCORE gained control of the Baja 1000, and in 1992 acquired the High

Desert Racing Association (HDRA), incorporating three of its races into SCORE's schedule. With this merger, Sal Fish became CEO of the HDRA, with its president Danny Cau (now retired) taking the same position for SCORE.

In 1995, ESPN, along with SCORE, developed the 'SCORE-Tecate Trophy Truck Series'. Created for television audiences, this format's wildly popular with the fans, both at home and on desert courses around the Southwest. Moving ever forward, SCORE welcomed Ivan 'Ironman' Stewart's new Pro Truck Racing Organization into the fold, again bringing fans more exciting racing action, and providing a true drivers' class for the racers.

Today, SCORE events are seen

around the world, with large television audiences in Japan and Europe, as well as North America. They receive regular coverage in newspapers and magazines, and on internet sites devoted to off-roading. The entertainment industry has taken notice of this exciting sport, creating video games, interactive CD-ROMs and a new 'motion simulator ride' based on the Pro Truck Racing Series.

As the sport branches out into new areas, it continues to grow in popularity and increase its market share in the world of motorsports. With a growing number of non-traditional sponsors augmenting mainstays like BF Goodrich and Toyota, SCORE-International is poised to take off-road racing into the next millennium.

Trophy Trucks

In 1993, SCORE was faced with the problem of creating an 'Unlimited' class of truck that the public could readily identify with. The solution was the 'Trophy Truck', and off-road racing would never be the same.

These thoroughbred racing machines represent the pinnacle of off-road racing technology, with engineering and design innovation rivaling that of any motorsport. Utilizing computer-aided design, composite alloys and metals like chromoly steel, magnesium and titanium, Trophy Trucks are among the finest of all motorsports exotica.

This level of professional racing requires factory or large corporate sponsorship, since the cost of the truck alone can exceed $300,000. When the costs of equipment, supplies, crew and support vehicles (including helicopter air support) are factored in, the total cost of a full racing season can total several million dollars.

Watching a Trophy Truck race is a breathtaking experience. The 5,500-pound vehicles are powered by 500+ cubic-inch engines, producing over 650 horsepower, and literally shake the ground when they pass by. Their passing, however, is often very brief, as Trophy Trucks have been clocked at speeds in excess of 140mph across open desert. When you consider that under the best of conditions, these trucks are racing in sand and loose gravel, the magnitude of that accomplishment becomes apparent. In the rougher sections of desert terrain, Trophy Trucks rely on over 28 inches of suspension travel and 37-inch tires to pull them through, to almost float over the toughest obstacles.

With three full seasons behind them, the Trophy Trucks have posted the fastest lap times and highest top speeds ever recorded in desert racing, thanks to the skill of drivers like 1994 Champion Rob MacCachren, 1995 winner Ivan 'Ironman' Stewart, and Robbie Gordon, 1996's victor. The ultimate success of Trophy Trucks, however, can be seen in the eyes of the fans, who fill the stands to capacity for a chance to see these warriors of the desert thunder by.

ROBBIE GORDON *1996's Trophy Truck champion with an uncommonly clean machine.*

Pro Trucks: The Future of Off-Road Racing

The most prohibitive factor in racing is its high cost. In the competitive world of off-road motorsports, the price of each piece of new technology, designed to make you that little bit faster than your opponents, quickly adds up. All too often, the result is a battle of checkbooks and wallets, rather trucks and their drivers. Ivan 'Ironman' Stewart and his new venture, The Pro Truck Racing Organization, intend to change all that, and the result could be the future of off-road racing.

In developing the Pro Truck format, Ivan looked at what other motorsports had to offer, and found what he was looking for in the concept of IROC. Having finalized the format, he began constructing a strong, lightweight truck using advanced technology, and parts manufactured by series sponsors, or their own shop. The Pro Truck's fiberglass body matches the engine manufacturer, keeping weight down, while adding a sense of brand loyalty the public can identify with. Stewart's overall design and construction give them peak performance, while keeping costs down, a key element of the Pro Truck philosophy.

Currently, the trucks are an official part of the SCORE Desert Racing Series, but Stewart sees that as only the beginning, since Pro Trucks are as capable of racing on short courses as they are in open desert. The Pro Truck concept, and the direction the sport in general, is best summarized by Ivan Stewart himself: "All we have done is tried to level the playing field to allow more drivers to be able to compete and have a chance to enjoy the same success that I have had in off-road racing. I truly believe that this is an opportunity for not only truck manufacturers to show and test their products, but also to have a true truck and driver champion."

THE LOW-DOWN ON PRO TRUCKS *Ivan Stewart is pushing these beasts to the fore of off-roading.*

OFF-ROAD IN THE USA

The Baja 1000

In the world of off-road motorsports, no event is as well known or challenging as the legendary Baja 1000. Held every November on the Baja California peninsula, the crown jewel of the SCORE Desert Racing Series attracts untold thousands of fans, hundreds of racers, and the undivided attention of viewing audiences around the world. Regarded by many as the ultimate test of man and machine, the Baja 1000 has earned itself a special place in racing history, alongside seminal events such as the Indy 500.

With roots going back to informal speed runs down the BC peninsula by luminaries like Bruce Meyers (creator of the legendary Meyers Manx), the event was officially established by the National Off-Road Racing Organization (NORRA) in 1967 as the Mexican 1000. In 1975, SCORE International took over NORRA's responsibilities, and the event became known as 'The Tecate SCORE Baja 1000'. Since that time, the course has been run over several areas, attracting participants from over 20 countries around the world. Over the years, contingents from England, Saudi Arabia, and exotic locales like New Caledonia have each accepted the challenge, with many returning year after year, determined to 'beat the Baja'.

The mystique surrounding the event is unequaled in the world of motorsports, and many have succumbed to its promise of adventure and fame. The Baja 1000 can be a harsh mistress, and for some there is only disappointment and frustration, as months of hard work and preparation are swept away by accident or mechanical failure. For others, it's a road to glory, bringing fame to the unknown, and establishing racers like Walker Evans, Ivan 'Ironman' Stewart, Roger Mears, and Rod Hall among the motorsport elite.

As we approach the new millennium, plans are underway for a celebratory event, scheduled to run from Tijuana to LaPaz... and back! The 'Baja 2000' is sure to be one of the greatest events in racing history, further adding to the legend that is The Baja.

DANGEROUS, INHOSPITABLE... FUN *The legendary Baja 1000 is another of this sport's conundrums.*

Baja Bugs

From the Baja California peninsula, where the vehicle takes its name, to the courses of the SCORE and FUD-Race Desert Series', the 'Baja Bug' has become a fixture of off-road motorsports. Easy and inexpensive to build, Baja Bugs start life as workaday Volkswagen Beetles, and undergo a dramatic transformation with the addition of fiberglass body panels, larger wheels and tires, and several other modifications, to become incredibly capable off-road performers.

Were Dr Porsche alive today, he too would stare in amazement at what his economically-designed 'people's car' is capable of when pushed to its limits. The SCORE Class 5-1600 cars are true racing vehicles, featuring chro-moly roll cages, long travel suspensions, and power output nearly double that of stock engines. Some of the greatest racers in off-road motorsports cut their teeth in the 5-1600 class before moving on, but like racing legend Carlos Iribe, many stay, as it remains one of the most competitive and challenging classes the sport has to offer.

The 5-1600's are about as far as you can push a Baja Bug and still consider it a true Volkswagen. Class 5 desert cars, however, are far beyond that. The very sight of one is enough to reduce a Volkswagen purist to tears. With wheel travel in the 20-inch range, full chro-moly chassis, and Porsche engines, it's no surprise fans and racers refer to these unlimited cars as 'Trophy Bugs'.

The Class 5 cars retain the general appearance of a Baja Bug, but their features are greatly exaggerated. The wheelbase and track width are several inches greater than that of their siblings in Class 5-1600; when combined with their much larger wheels and tires, the result is an intimidating appearance. Engine output of the Class 5s can approach 250 horsepower—considering that the total weight of the car is well under 2,000 pounds, the power-to-weight ratio rivals that of Trophy Trucks.

THE PEOPLE'S CAR *The off-road evolution of the VW Beetle has created many ingenious hybrids.*

Off-Road Motorcycles

Off-road motorcycles can be traced back to World War I, when motorcycle sidecars were in wide use as transport and reconnaissance vehicles in several conflicts. The sport of off-road motorcycling, or dirt biking, first became popular in the late 1960s and early '70s, propelled by the talents of riders like Roger DeCoster, and journalists like Rick Seiman, who gave the sport a wide American audience. In following years, off-road motorcycles have steadily grown in popularity and performance, with enthusiasts gravitating toward specific types of riding.

The twisting, mud-filled trails, common to the forests and mountains, are a favorite of many eastern riders. The feeling of freedom afforded by a motorcycle is a perfect complement to the fresh air and breathtaking scenery of the American wilderness. Desert and dune riding are popular in the west, and because of mild winter temperatures, can be enjoyed all year around.

One trend that these different areas share is the move toward the use of four-stroke engines. Environmental concerns and increasing emission controls are slowly ending the reign of the once-dominant two-stroke; California has banned two-stroke vehicles produced after January 1997 from its public lands.

One place that a two-stroke may never be replaced, however, is on the tracks of the American Motorcyclist Association (AMA) 'Supercross' Series. Filling stadiums around the country with tens of thousands of screaming fans, Supercross is a tour de force of action and excitement, representing the pinnacle of dirt bike technology. In this fast-paced world, a good showing by an independent motorcyclist can result in a factory ride, but for the factories themselves, the stakes are much higher. The old adage of 'Win on Sunday, sell on Monday' holds true: event wins translate directly into product sales, continuing the trend by bringing more riders into the sport.

ABOVE: DIFFERENT STROKES *Environmentalists are pressing for a two-stroke ban.*

OVER: PLAIN SALES *Victory in the AMA stakes can translate directly into more sales for manufacturers.*

Open-Wheeled Cars

Open-wheeled cars come in a variety of forms, and have been a staple of off-roading since the sport began. Originally created by removing the body from a VW Beetle, leaving only the chassis and powertrain, the result was a light car, better suited for play in the soft sands and rocky conditions of the American Southwest. As time went on, stronger tubular steel chassis' were constructed, utilizing lightweight, reliable VW engine and suspension components, along with several custom-fabricated pieces, designed to maximize performance.

Over the years, two distinct types of open-wheel cars have evolved to meet the differing needs of off-roaders and their terrain of preference. The first are 'Sand Rails', built for the soft, blow-sand conditions found at dunes and beaches. The Sand Rails' light weight and high horsepower make them as capable of flying over the tallest dunes of Glamis, California, as they are at tearing up the strip at Michigan's Silver Lake Sand Dragway.

The second type are known as 'Desert' or 'Rock Rails', and are built for the demanding conditions found in the open desert and mountains. These cars emphasize strength and reliability over weight and speed, having much in common with the desert racers of SCORE.

The open-wheel cars of the SCORE Desert Racing Series—buggies—are some of the most amazing vehicles in off-road motorsports. When 'piloted' by skilled drivers like John Herder and Troy Herbst, Class 1 cars have taken on, and occasionally beaten, the mighty Trophy Trucks for the 'Overall' title at racing events like the 1997 Parker 400.

Exotics in their own right, these cars feature a chro-moly chassis, carbon fiber body panels, and state-of-the-art onboard navigation systems. With well over 20 inches of wheel travel, and aluminum six-cylinder engines producing in excess of 300 horsepower, the open-wheeled Class 1 cars are among the fastest vehicles in the sport.

Pre-Runners

Asphalt racers have the luxury of inspecting a course during practice laps, but things work a bit differently in off-road racing. These courses of sand and loose gravel can be a thousand miles long, and their conditions change with the passing of each vehicle. Considering the great distances involved, as well as the number of variables, it's impossible to know what the course's condition will be when it's time to race.

Pre-running the course does, however, give the racer a reasonable idea of what he's up against, and where accidents are likely to happen. It also allows teams to find the best place for secondary pit areas, enabling support crews to quickly respond to a disabled race vehicle, should trouble arise. Pre-running the course in the actual race vehicle is not recommended, due to the punishment that these courses inflict on equipment. The solution is called, simply, a 'Pre-Runner'.

Pre-Runners can be open-wheeled, tube chassis cars, or modified trucks, with wheel travel, suspension, and power similar to that of a race vehicle. Built to take on desert terrain at close to competition speed, they differ from their faster siblings in that they include creature comforts for their occupants, as many long hours are spent mapping the course. Standard equipment for many Pre-Runners include multiple seats, coolers, and food warmers, along with communication and navigational equipment.

In addition to their scouting duties, Pre-Runners also serve as 'chase' vehicles, bringing tools and spare parts to racers unable to reach a primary or secondary pit for assistance. Equipped for chase duty, they're often loaded with portable compressors, welders, and other items needed to make a variety of field repairs. The chase crew is an invaluable part of a team's racing effort, and on more than one occasion have turned a DNF (did not finish) into the sweet taste of victory.

VEGAS STAKES *Events at places such as Las Vegas are putting all forms of off-roading on the map.*

Recreational Trucks

Recreational off-roading is the 'meat and potatoes' of this motorsport, and while there are many ways to enjoy it, the most popular is in a truck. Like all performance enthusiasts, off-roaders are never satisfied with standard factory models, and set about transforming their trucks into the 'go anywhere, do anything' vehicles of their dreams.

While each truck is as individual as its driver, they all have several things in common.

The first step on the path from stock truck to recreational truck is usually larger wheels and tires. Offering superior traction and ground clearance, they can be the most important modification you make.

Depending on the size of the tires and the user's needs, or both, the next step is often a suspension lift, with larger shock absorbers. Stock suspension, as delivered from the factory, is rarely adequate for off-road use, and many off-roaders upgrade it with one of the kits available on the market.

Auxiliary lights on a bed-mounted 'roll' or light bar are a popular addition, as are lamps secured to a front-mounted brush guard. Whether you enjoy nighttime off-roading, or want them 'just in case', they're far superior to a truck's standard halogen headlights, and improve the off-road look of the vehicle.

From this point on, things get very expensive. The only limits to what you can do are your imagination and, of course, your wallet. Winches, locking differentials, exotic suspensions, and frame-mounted tubular steel roll cages capable of supporting a truck's weight, are all high-dollar items essential for a hard-core trail machine, but optional for recreational use.

Properly built recreational trucks are perfect for weekend trips to the mountains, camping, or other family outings, and can handle the challenges of moderate off-road terrain. They retain a high level of drive-ability, without the hassles associated with hardcore trail vehicles.

Rock Crawling

Rock-crawling in the Sierra Nevada mountains may well be the ultimate example of 'because it's there' mentality. What else would possess people to traverse terrain filled with jagged boulders larger than their vehicles, at speeds averaging less than one mph? This sport demands supreme finesse and vehicular control, as one wrong move can send you plummeting down the side of a mountain, or at the very least, leave you with an enormous repair bill, and the embarrassment of returning home on a tow strap.

Perhaps the most famous rock-crawling trail is the Rubicon. Located near Lake Tahoe in northern California, this ten-mile course is perhaps better measured in hours, as it can take up to two full days to cross. Conditions vary widely, as spring run-off from the winter snows change the face and character of the trail, year by year. Even at its easiest, it's not a trail for stock or general usage trucks. The Rubicon requires machines built for the purpose, if they're to have any chance at seeing the other side under their own power.

The trucks of choice are Jeep CJs and the Toyota Land Cruiser FJ series. While outstanding vehicles in stock form, it takes a lot of work to turn them into 'crawlers'. Increased ground clearance is a must—the trucks are equipped with 33–35-inch tires and several inches of suspension lift.

Torque is first multiplied through a transmission and transfer case, equipped with extremely low gearing (75:1 or lower), keeping the engine in its powerband, while 'crawling' over the trail's many obstacles. It's hard to get traction over the uneven terrain, so positive locking differentials are installed to send the engine's torque to all four wheels evenly.

A big winch and 'body armor' round out the package, and give the rock crawler an added measure of insurance for those times when 'Just a little more', should have been 'Back up and try it again'.

OVER: BUMP AND GRIND *Rock crawling is one of the most bone-shaking sports around.*

DESERT RATS *Crossing the shifting sands is an awesome sight and a monumental task.*

Sand Sports

Sand vehicles have come a long way since an enterprising man named Scott McKenzie modified a VW Beetle for better performance among the dunes. Today, a typical weekend at Southern California hot spots like the Imperial Sand Dunes near Glamis includes jeeps, Broncos, ATVs, dirt bikes, and Sand Rails, as well as radical custom-built machines which defy categorization. Variety is the duners' spice of life, a fact reflected in the variety of vehicles they drive.

Big weekends like Thanksgiving and New Year's Eve draw over 200,000 people to the dunes, making it the world's largest motorized event. Overnight, the surrounding area becomes a virtual city of RVs and campers, complete with a full complement of vendors to serve the temporary occupants' needs in these remote areas.

The days at Glamis are filled with the smell of race fuel and the high-pitched shriek of two-stroke engines tuned within an inch of their life. Dirt bikes and ATVs fly over razorback dunes, with enough daring and bravado to make Robbie Kenevel jealous. Not to be outdone, sand cars, and trucks, powered by blown, injected, alcohol-burning motors, accelerate across the dunes like NHRA dragsters.

At night, 'Competition Hill' becomes the center of attention as 'The World's Largest Light and Sound Show' gets underway. Crowds of people line the dunes, as vehicles sporting everything from neon to Christmas lights thunder up the hill in an amazing display of raw horsepower and showmanship. Vehicles often wait in line for hours for their shot at Competition Hill, and when that chance comes, you can be sure they make the best of it.

Sand sports are among the most popular of all off-road motorsports today, thanks to innovators like Mike Mazzone and Ron Lummus, who push the modern sand vehicles farther than ever thought possible. It's a rare person indeed who isn't hooked on the sport from his first ride in the dunes.

ATV? IT HAD BETTER BE! *The roughest riding and the least protection are offered by ATV sand sports.*

DRIVERS

Throughout the history of American motorsports, there have been those who have left an indelible mark, setting standards for others to follow, and goals for them to achieve. The sport of off-road racing is fortunate in claiming many of these notable people as its own.

In the world of off-road motorcycle racing, pioneers like J. N. Roberts and Roger DeCoster set, broke, and reset records as they pushed their early motocross and desert bikes to the limit. Bob 'Hurricane' Hannah and the legendary Yamaha YZ factory bikes redefined the concept of what a rider and bike could be, winning multiple AMA Championships —among others—before retiring in the mid-1980s. Hannah's exciting, out-of-control riding style was practically made for TV, and increased coverage of the sport by the networks. The factory YZs which Hannah took to victory were unique for their time, and introduced the single rear shock concept to the racing world.

The most significant contribution to the sport during its early years was not made by a famous racer, or a revolutionary motorcycle. It came from a journalist named Rick Seiman, and a magazine called *Dirt Bike*. Considered to be 'The Bible' by many racers, as well as recreational riders, the publication's informative articles, thorough race coverage, and honest product reviews determined the direction the entire sport has since taken.

Larry Roseler

Desert rider Larry Roseler amassed a string of victories and championships during the 1980s and '90s, which many feel will never be equalled. Retiring from motorcycle racing at the peak of his career in the mid-'90s, but harboring a great love of the desert, Roseler crossed over into four-wheeled motorsports, currently driving the McPherson Class 7 Chevrolet in the SCORE Desert Racing Series.

Parnelli Jones

The early 1970s saw Indy car legend Parnelli Jones cross over into desert racing, pitting himself and his Ford Bronco against the Baja 1000. Of the asphalt racers who've made the transition, Jones is one of the few to do so with great success. He returned to Indy cars, but his accomplishments in the world of off-road racing are a rich part of its history.

Roger Mears

Roger Mears also found great success in the desert before moving onto asphalt. A five-time Baja 1000 Champion (1979, 1980, 1986, 1989, and 1991), Mears won two HDRA/SCORE Desert Championships (1989 and 1991), with victory at 20 World Championship events.

Popular with fans and racers alike, Mears and his trucks were featured in a Hollywood production about off-road racing in the late 1980s.

Rod Hall

Rod Hall has made major contributions to off-road racing history since his career began behind the wheel of a World War II vintage jeep. Winning hundreds of individual events throughout the Southwest, Hall holds the record of 15 victories at the Baja 1000, and has participated in every race since the inaugural 1967 running.

Hall stands alone as the only man to win the Overall title at the Baja 1000 in a four-wheel-drive vehicle.

Walker Evans

Walker Evans and his brightly-colored Dodge trucks were a dominant force during the 1980s and early '90s, amassing numerous wins in Class 8. Suspension design on the Barbary Coast-sponsored vehicles were highly influential, and helped Evans achieve some of the highest speeds desert racing had seen. Before retiring from active competition, to pursue the sport's business and managerial aspects, Evans competed in the SCORE Trophy Truck series, finishing his stellar career in desert racing's premier class.

ROGER MEARS *A star of SCORE and screen.*

Carlos Iribe

Mexican driver Carlos Iribe entered the sport in 1977 from a career in Trans-Am and Formula 'A' competition and has been near or at the top of every class he's since raced in. With well over 200 off-road wins to his credit, including victories at the Baja 500 and 1000, his winning ways continue in SCORE's Class 5-1600, at the wheel of the ISRT Baja Bug.

Iribe holds a 'Baja Spirit' award, presented to those who 'represent the spirit of Baja' (good sportsmanship and willingness to help fellow competitors), and is highly regarded by his peers. To quote SCORE CEO Sal Fish, "Guys like Carlos *are* off-road racing."

Larry Ragland

'Lightning' Larry Ragland continues to enjoy a career which has encompassed 30 event victories and seven championship titles since he began astride a motorcycle in 1976. Ragland has raced in a variety of classes, including Class 1 open wheel cars, Class 7 mini-trucks, Class 8 full-size trucks, and currently in the SCORE Trophy Truck Series, where his Chevrolet K/1500 has won two consecutive Baja 1000 Championships.

Wildly popular with American and Mexican race fans, Larry Ragland has inspired many to enter the sport, and has proved to be one of its true ambassadors.

Ivan Stewart

Oklahoma native Ivan Stewart is undoubtedly one of the finest drivers to ever cross a finish line, as well as one of the most popular. At races across the American southwest and Mexico, this consummate professional is surrounded by enthusiastic fans who come to see the 'Ironman' in person. Gracious as always, he signs autographs and poses for pictures with an unforced smile and a gleam in his eye.

Outside the sport, Stewart is very active in the community, working with organizations like the Make-A-Wish Foundation and Special Olympics. A hero to many children, he visits schools in southern California, encouraging kids to continue their education and follow their dreams.

Stewart's racing career began in 1973, and while that event was in the first of many victories throughout the '70s, the best was yet to come. In 1983, Stewart joined the Toyota factory sponsored team, and took a total of 17 Grand National Sport Truck wins and three GNST championships in The Mickey Thompson Off-Road Stadium Racing Series. Along with his teammates, Stewart helped propel Toyota to 42 main event victories and 11 manufacturer championships; three times that of any other truck.

All told, Stewart's 25 years in the sport have so far resulted in 80 career victories, including eight Driver Championships in both Stadium and Desert Racing. Highlights of that illustrious, ongoing career include wins in 13 Baja 500s, eight Mint 400s, four Parker 400s and two Baja 1000s. His many solo victories in the Baja races have rightfully earned him the name 'Ironman'.

While he continues to compete in selected SCORE events as the sole driver of the Toyota Trophy Truck, Stewart has entered the world of race promotion, with the launch of the Pro Truck Racing Organization. The series, which came from his desire to make the sport more affordable and accessible, has captured the attention of some of the biggest names in motorsports sponsorship, and has further solidified the status of Ivan 'Ironman' Stewart as a legend in the world of off-road motorsports.

LARRY RAGLAND *One of off-roading's ambassadors.*

IVAN STEWART *A good driver, a popular man and a visionary innovator.*

SPORTS CAR RACING

To some traditionalists, the era of REAL sports car racing in North America began and ended with the Canadian-American Challenge Cup series—the Can-Am—of the late 1960s and early '70s, when a glorious variety of seemingly unlimited, primarily V8-powered cars provided spectacular competition among some of the world's top drivers. Others go back a little further in time, to the 1950s, when the likes of Briggs Cunningham and Carroll Shelby produced cars to challenge—and briefly vanquish—the established might of European marques such as Aston Martin, Ferrari, Jaguar, and Maserati.

Younger aficionados, meanwhile, may prefer to dwell on the silhouette-bodied Group 5 cars of the mid-70s, when a series of ever more outrageous developments of the relatively humble Porsche 911 ruled the roost in competitions hosted by the International Motor Sports Association (IMSA); or a little later when sports prototype machines such as the Lola T-600 and, subsequently, Group C Porsches, Nissans and Jaguars were joined in battle on classical road racing venues all across the country.

Then again, some might say today's breed of World Sports Cars represent the top of the tree. Certainly, the fresh outlook provided by Professional SportsCar Racing Inc (*SportsCar*), led by new owner Andy Evans, who took over the sanctioning duties from IMSA in early 1997, seemed to pay dividends right away as record fields and large crowds gathered for North America's two premier sports car events in Florida—the Rolex 24 at Daytona and the Sebring 12 Hours.

The term 'sports car racing' effectively covers a multitude of disciplines and championships. Today, SportsCar's Exxon Supreme World Sports Car Championship caters for a broad spectrum of open-topped prototype cars, and runs in conjunction with three separate GT categories featuring production-based automobiles. The rival Sports Car Club of America, meanwhile, which for many years after its foundation in 1944 retained, somewhat controversially, a strict amateur status, eventually bowed to the pressure of encroaching professionalism and now counts the Trans-Am Championship as its flagship series.

Critics might argue that the 'muscle cars' (as they became known during the 1960s and '70s) aren't sports cars at all—merely modified sedans—but the fact is that the Trans-Am series has provided the backbone of SCCA Pro Racing for more than 30 years. It has also provided valuable recognition for some of America's best known drivers, among them Mark Donohue, Parnelli Jones, George Follmer and, more recently, the likes of Scott Pruett, Tom Kendall, and Scott Sharp.

The SCCA's roots continue to be served by a plethora of categories which attract amateur drivers to events throughout the United States. Once a year, the top protagonists from every category and each of 11 geographical regions are invited to the famed SCCA Valvoline Runoffs to determine who shall have the right to be crowned as 'National Champion.'

Commencing in 1964, the SCCA Runoffs—or the American Road Race of Champions, as it was originally termed—alternated between Daytona International Speedway, Florida, and the sadly lamented Riverside International Raceway, California. The event, which routinely draws more than 500 competitors, was switched to Road Atlanta, Georgia in 1970, where it remained until settling on its present location at the equally scenic and challenging Mid-Ohio Sports Car Course in 1994.

DAYTONA *Once a key SCCA track, it now hosts the Rolex 24, one of the sport's premier events.*

THE HISTORY

In terms of international significance—and despite the early efforts of pioneer promoters such as James Gordon Bennett and William K. Vanderbilt—auto racing in North America revolved almost exclusively around oval track racing and, particularly, the Indianapolis 500. This state of affairs persisted until the early 1950s.

Other forms of motor sport grew in a rather haphazard form. Nevertheless, having hosted the early Vanderbilt Cup races, Long Island, NY, also played a major role in the development of sports car racing. During the 1920s and '30s, as European manufacturers left their American counterparts far behind in terms of developing the automobile beyond a mere utilitarian form, some of the more affluent Northeasterners began to look farther afield both for diversity and fulfillment of their sporting instincts. Naturally enough, the urge to compete followed soon after.

Wealthy brothers Miles and Sam Collier joined other like-minded souls in the 1930s to form the grandly titled Automobile Racing Club of America, and for a decade ARCA hosted events all over New England. The format remained loose, and strictly amateur. A wide variety of cars was attracted, ranging from virtually stock European imports to a bizarre selection of hybrids such as Briggs Cunningham's BuMerc, featuring the chassis and engine from a Buick Century clad with the body from a crashed Mercedes SSK.

After World War II effectively brought ARCA to an end, many former members reconvened with others to form the Sports Car Club of America. The inaugural SCCA meeting was held on February 26, 1944, in the Boston home of Chapin Wallour, where the club defined its purpose: "To further the preservation and operation of sports cars, to act as an authentic source of information thereupon and to provide events for these cars and their owners." Theodore F. Robertson was elected as the SCCA's first president. Shortly afterward, he initiated publication of a club magazine, entitled *Sportwagen*, although before too

PIONEER SPIRIT *The Vanderbilt Race, seen here in 1937.*

long it had assumed a more anglicized moniker, *SportsCar*, which remains to this day.

The SCCA's first major event, on October 2, 1948, was held at Watkins Glen, NY, and was won by Frank Griswold's pre-war Alfa Romeo. Briggs Cunningham claimed second in his aging BuMerc. Coincidentally, the final ARCA event, held at the New York World's Fair in 1940, had seen an almost identical result, except that Cunningham's car on that occasion had been driven by close friend Miles Collier.

The SCCA soon began to flourish, spreading its sphere of influence throughout the country. The club, which now boasts well over 50,000 members, retained its base in New England for the first 29 years, before relocating to Englewood, a southern suburb of Denver, Colorado, in 1972.

The abiding credo of the SCCA, however, was to retain the sport's amateur status, and as other sanctioning bodies such as USAC (Indy car racing) and NASCAR (stock car racing) began to grow in stature and host more prestigious events, so the sports car world was left behind—at least in terms of

OPPOSITE: *The Trans-Am, born in 1966, still flourishes today.*

156

international significance. There were plenty of talented race car drivers and gifted engineers in the United States, but only rarely were they able to earn any compensation for their efforts or become recognized outside their homeland.

The first sign of change came in 1953, when the governing body of world motor sport, the Paris, France-based Federation Internationale de l'Automobile (FIA), established the World Sports Car Championship. The fledgling series comprised the world's most prestigious endurance events, namely the Le Mans 24 Hours (France), Mille Miglia (Italy), Spa 24 Hours (Belgium), Nurburgring 1000 Kms (Germany), Dundrod Tourist Trophy (Northern Ireland), and the Carrera Panamericana (Mexico). The opening event, however, on March 8, 1953, was the 12 Hours of Sebring, and against all the odds—not to mention the factory-backed European teams—John Fitch and Phil Walters guided their 5.4-liter Chrysler V8-engined Cunningham C-4R to a famous victory.

The annual event at Sebring remained as North America's umbilical cord to the outside world for almost a decade. Nevertheless, in the intervening period, drivers such as Phil Hill, Richie Ginther, and Dan Gurney cut their teeth in SCCA competition before setting their sights on Formula 1.

Unfortunately, the Americans became even more isolated in 1957 when the FIA introduced an arbitrary 3.0-liter limit on engine size. The local V8 machinery was effectively outlawed overnight.

The following summer, however, the United States Auto Club (USAC) grasped an opportunity to put American road racing back on the map by promoting a brand new event, the US Grand Prix for Sports Cars, at Riverside, California. A hefty (for the time) prize fund of almost $15,000 attracted many top names, including several Indy Car drivers. The race was won by Chuck Daigh in one of Lance Reventlow's locally-built, Chevrolet-powered Scarabs.

Spurred on by the success of the USAC event at Riverside, the SCCA finally began to cave in to pressure from its members. The first money-paying events hosted by the SCCA were held in 1958, although it wasn't until '63 that the first fully-fledged professional series emerged in the form of the United States Road Racing Championship (USRRC).

By then, of course, the rear- or, to be more precise, mid-engined revolution was virtually complete. The wholesale transition from front-engined machinery had begun in Formula 1 in 1957, when the British firm, Cooper, fitted an enlarged Coventry-Climax FPF engine to a version of its successful range of Formula Junior, F3, and F2 cars. Jack Brabham was entrusted with the car. Two years later, the Australian won the first of his three world championship titles. Cooper's small-engined 'Bob-tail' emulated the trend in sports cars during the middle 1950s.

Several American customers soon seized upon the idea of installing small-block V8 motors in a mid-engined chassis, although none were as adventurous—or as controversial—as Roger Penske, who, in 1962, rebuilt a crashed F1 Cooper beneath a full-width body and fitted a larger 2.7-liter Climax engine. As if that wasn't enough, Penske attracted support from the DuPont Company and christened his creation the 'Zerex Special.' Sponsorship was up and running.

By 1966, the USRRC had evolved into the first Canadian-American Challenge Cup Series which was sanctioned jointly by the SCCA and the Canadian Automobile Sport Clubs (CASC). That same year, the SCCA also introduced its Trans-American Sedan Championship—the Trans-Am.

The Can-Am series, complying with the FIA's new Group 7 'two-seater unrestricted sports car' category, soon began to attract some exotic machinery. The Trans-Am, too, developed rapidly. Austrian Formula 1 driver Jochen Rindt claimed victory in the first-ever Trans-Am race at Sebring, but it rapidly became the domain of American drivers such as Mark Donohue, Jerry Titus, George Follmer, and 1963 Indianapolis 500 winner Parnelli Jones.

While the Trans-Am has continued to this day, the Can-Am's glittering early success led to spiralling costs which eventually caused its abandonment at the end of the 1974 season. The series was reincarnated in 1977 and continued, somewhat spasmodically, until 1986, when the concept was abandoned for good.

In the meantime, disgruntled former SCCA stalwart John Bishop had struck out on his own in 1969 to form the International Motor Sports Association. The first race offered a purse of $3,000 and attracted just 348 spectators, but IMSA soon grew from that modest beginning.

Bishop inaugurated a six-race Grand Touring (GT) Championship in 1971, which the following year enjoyed the start of a long and lucrative sponsorship from the Camel brand of R.J. Reynolds Tobacco. The IMSA Camel GT Championship was initially open to cars conforming to the FIA's Group 4 category, although following the lead of NASCAR's Bill France, Bishop reserved the right to make modifications to the regulations in order to ensure close competition. A switch to the less restricted Group 5 cars enabled IMSA to come into line with the FIA's World Championship of Makes (the latest incarnation of the former World Sports Car Championship) in the mid-1970s, while 1981 saw the series move over toward true sports prototypes as Brian Redman claimed the spoils aboard a Lola T-600.

A fresh breed of Group C prototypes was introduced by the FIA for the renamed (again) World Endurance Championship in 1982. These cars soon became the staple of IMSA's Camel GT series, albeit supported, as are today's breed of World Sports Cars, by various classes for production-based cars.

CHEQUERED HISTORY *John Surtees seen here winning the 1966 Can-Am; a race which floundered in 1974, recovered 1974 and was finally laid to rest in 1986.*

THE DRIVERS

Geoff Brabham

The eldest son of three time Formula 1 world champion Sir Jack Brabham, who spawned the 'rear-engined revolution' at Indianapolis after running strongly for Cooper in 1961, Geoff raced successfully both in his native Australia and in Europe before moving to the United States in 1978. That's when his career really took off. He won the SCCA Super Vee title in 1979 and added the Can-Am crown—for Team VDS—in 1981.

Brabham never managed to win an Indy Car race in 89 starts, despite finishing second six times, but he became a dominant force in IMSA competition as he scooped a record four consecutive championships for the factory Nissan team from 1988–91.

Mark Donohue

The New Jersey native began his competitive career while still at school by entering—and winning—a hillclimb with his Chevrolet Corvette. After achieving success with the SCCA in an Elva Courier and a TVR, among other cars, the graduate engineer was catapulted to stardom when he joined forces with Roger Penske in the middle 1960s.

Donohue won USRRC titles in 1967 and '68, then set his sights on the Trans-Am series, scoring an incredible 29 victories from just 55 starts between 1968 and '71. His win tally remains unsurpassed. 'Captain Nice' was equally successful in Indy cars, winning the Indianapolis 500 in 1972, and the Can-Am, taking six straight races and the championship in 1973.

Tragically, after switching to Formula 1, the 38-year-old lost his life following a crash prior to the Austrian Grand Prix in 1975.

Jim Downing

'Gentleman Jim' Downing, an IMSA stalwart since 1978, was largely instrumental in instigating the Camel Lights division for smaller, relatively inexpensive cars to run alongside the GT prototypes (GTP) in 1985. The quietly-spoken, bespectacled Atlanta native went on to win the first three Camel Lights titles to add to his earlier GTU championship in 1982. All came at the wheel of Mazda-powered cars.

Juan Fangio II

Consecutive IMSA GT Prototype championship titles in 1992 and '93, driving Dan Gurney's All American Racers GTP Eagle-Toyota, showed that Fangio was no lightweight driver—even by comparison with his famous uncle, Juan Manuel Fangio, who was a dominant force in the 1950s, claiming a record five world championships.

The younger Fangio achieved success at home in Argentina, but before following in his uncle's footsteps and heading for Europe in the early 1980s, Juan II showed his versatility both there and on subsequent visits to North America, and in 1986 he established the beginning of a successful partnership with Gurney, one of his uncle's great friends and rivals.

MARK DONOHUE *aka 'Captain Nice' has an unsurpassed record in Trans-Am.*

George Follmer

Follmer was an insurance broker before turning his attention to auto racing. Already 25 when he began autocrossing in 1959, the Californian would not race professionally for another five years. Success, though, came quickly. After scoring six class wins and the outright USRRC crown in 1965 with a Porsche-powered Lotus 23, Follmer graduated into the Can-Am.

Follmer displayed his bravery aboard Trevor Harris's astonishing 'tiny tire' AVS Shadow in 1970, then dominated the series in 1972 with Roger Penske's 'turbo Panzer' Porsche 917/10K. Follmer also won in Indy cars and the Trans-Am, clinching the title in 1972 for AMC Javelin and again

for Porsche in '76. He raced one season in Formula 1 for UOP Shadow, with a best finish of third in the 1973 Spanish GP.

Peter Gregg

Sharing a Porsche 914 with long-time partner Hurley Haywood, Gregg won the first-ever IMSA GT race on April 18, 1971, at Virginia International Raceway—and went on to become one of the most successful drivers in IMSA history. His tally of 41 victories, all except two in Porsches, ranks second only to Al Holbert. Gregg and Haywood shared the first-ever GTU title (for under-3.0 liter cars) but Gregg won six more crowns for his Brumos team. He also won 20 races and two titles in SCCA Trans-

PHIL HILL *America's first F1 champ was adept at many disciplines.*

Am competition with a trusty Porsche Carrera.

Peter Gregg was equally successful in business, establishing a thriving Porsche, VW, and Audi distributorship in his native town of Jacksonville, Florida, which made his suicide shortly after marrying his fiancée, Deborah, all the more unfathomable.

Hurley Haywood

While many of Haywood's 34 IMSA victories were achieved with Peter Gregg, he was also a frequent winner in his own right. Haywood has spent most of his career in sports cars—almost exclusively with Porsche—although he did turn his hand briefly to Indy cars and raced once at the Indianapolis 500, placing 18th in 1980.

In addition to his two IMSA GT Championships, Haywood has accumulated a remarkable record in long-distance events, after winning Le Mans twice, Sebring twice, and the Daytona 24 Hours an amazing five times. Other successes include the 1988 Trans-Am title, driving the spectacular four-wheel-drive Audi 200 Turbo Quattro, and the 1991 Bridgestone Supercar Championship in a Brumos Porsche 911 Turbo.

Phil Hill

Prior to becoming America's first Formula 1 World Champion in 1961, at the wheel of the evocative 'shark-nose' Ferrari 156, Hill had begun his career in 1950, racing an MG TC on the West Coast. He soon graduated into a succession of Ferraris and, after finishing second in the 1956 Buenos Aires 1000 Kms, was offered a contract with the factory team in Europe.

Hill's successes include three wins in the 12 Hours of Sebring and two at the Le Mans 24 Hours. He also won for Jim Hall's Chaparral team in the twilight of his career, taking the high-winged 2E to victory in a 1966 Can-Am race at Riverside and an equally memorable triumph with the gorgeous 2F at Brands Hatch the following year.

Al Holbert/ Bob Holbert

Bob Holbert was a tremendously successful sports car exponent, especially with the factory Porsche team in the late 1950s and '60s. He claimed the first USRRC crown in

GEORGER FOLLMER *Former insurance broker and Indy, Trans-Am, and Can-Am winner.*

1963, driving both a Porsche and one of Carroll Shelby's 'King Cobras.'

It was only natural that his son should follow in his footsteps, and Al, too, became synonymous with Porsche, winning his first ever race in a 914/6 in 1971 and going on to win a record 49 IMSA Camel GT races and five championships—second only to Peter Gregg.

Holbert became Porsche's director of North American motor sport and was busily preparing an onslaught on the Indy Car champ-ionship when he was killed in a plane crash in 1988, at the age of 41.

Denis Hulme

'Denny the Bear,' as the sometimes grumpy New Zealander was affectionately known, is remembered as much for his exploits in the halcyon days of the Can-Am as for winning the Formula 1 World Championship in 1967.

Hulme worked his way up the auto racing ladder by winning a 'Driver to Europe' award in 1960, then plying his trade as a mechanic. He joined forces with fellow Kiwi Bruce McLaren in 1968, winning twice in F1, and continued with the team until the end of the 1974 season.

The 'Bruce and Denny Show' dominated Can-Am competition between 1967 and '72. Hulme won two championships and a record 22 races. He died of a heart attack during a race at Bathurst, Australia in 1992—but not before bringing his BMW safely to a halt. He was 56.

Tom Kendall

Yet another second generation racer, 'TK' grew up around the sport and soon immersed himself in it. By the end of the 1996 season, at just 30 years of age, Kendall already had nine professional championships under his belt, including three in the IMSA GTU division—he was the youngest ever IMSA champion, aged just 19, in 1986—and three in the SCCA Trans-Am series, including two straight for Jack Roush's factory-backed Ford Mustang Cobras in 1995 and '96.

Bruce McLaren

The other half of the 'Bruce and Denny Show,' McLaren, like Hulme, travelled to Europe after winning a 'scholarship' from the New Zealand Grand Prix Association. McLaren hooked up with Aussie Jack Brabham upon his arrival in England, and the kindred spirits spent several years with Cooper before establishing their own teams and building their own cars in Formula 1.

McLaren's first F1 win had come at the US Grand Prix at Sebring in 1959, at the tender age of 22. It was a harbinger of things to come, for McLaren reaped great success in North America, both as a driver and a chassis designer/ manufacturer. The quiet Kiwi's career was tragically cut short, killed while testing his newest Can-Am challenger at Goodwood, England, in June 1970.

Bob Sharp/ Scott Sharp

After claiming six SCCA championships for Datsun in the late 1960s and early '70s, as well as an IMSA GTU crown in 1975, Bob Sharp took the responsibility for guiding his friend, movie star Paul Newman, into the sport. Fittingly, Newman added another four SCCA titles, while Bob's son, Scott, kept the streak alive as he grabbed three more of his own.

The younger Sharp went on to win the 1991 Trans-Am championship with Buz McCall's factory-backed Chevrolet Camaro, then graduated into the Indy cars and was co-champion of the Indy Racing League in its inaugural season, 1996, driving for the legendary A.J. Foyt.

Wayne Taylor

After a promising career driving single-seaters in his native South Africa, Taylor began concentrating on sports cars in the late 1980s, initially in Europe, before settling in the United States.

Taylor scored his first IMSA victory with a Chevrolet-engined Intrepid at a soggy New Orleans in 1991. He became the inaugural World Sports Car champion in 1994, despite not winning a single race while sharing Jim Downing's ultra-reliable Mazda-powered Kudzu DG-3. He added a second WSC crown in '96, this time winning four times in an Oldsmobile Aurora-engined Riley & Scott Mk.III.

Bob Tullius

Founder (with Brian Fuerstenau) of the famed Group 44 Inc team based in Winchester, Virginia, Tullius was among the first to exploit the commercial opportunities within the amateur ranks of the SCCA. In 1961, while employed as a salesman with Kodak, the brusque, crewcut Tullius persuaded Standard-Triumph to give him a brand-new Triumph TR4. He duly won four straight E-Production championships.

Tullius was equally successful after switching to Jaguar, first with an E-Type in SCCA national competition, then adding two Trans-Am titles with an XJ-S in 1977 and '78. Tullius guided Jaguar into the IMSA GTP arena with the gorgeous Lee Dykstra-designed XJR-5 and finished second in the 1983 standings after winning four times.

BRUCE MCLAREN *Tragedy struck as he tested his new Can-Am racer in 1970.*

THE CARS

Chaparral

An accomplished driver—he won the USRRC in 1964—Jim Hall also proved to be an extraordinarily gifted and innovative engineer. Hall, in conjunction with his close friend and partner 'Hap' Sharp, built their Chaparral cars in Midland, Texas, and pioneered several aspects of race car design, including automatic transmission (fitted in the Chaparral 2A), aerodynamic wings (starting with the 2C), and ground-effects (the bizarre 2J 'sucker car,' which featured an auxiliary snowmobile engine mounted above the transmission to evacuate air from the engine bay and create a low-pressure area beneath the car).

Most of Hall's creations—some of them introduced in a fruitful partnership with General Motors —were outlawed at one time or another, but the man was truly a genius despite this frustrating treatment.

CHAPARRAL *All of Jim Hall's cars were innovative and this is no exception.*

race of all: the Le Mans 24 Hours.

He tried first in 1950 with a pair of almost stock Cadillacs and returned the following year with the Cunningham C-2R, built in West Palm Beach, Florida and powered by a 5425cc Chrysler V8. A C-3R won at Sebring in 1953 and recorded a best finish of third at Le Mans. Similar cars were successful in national events throughout the '50s.

Cunningham

Cincinnati-born Briggs Swift Cunningham had the financial wherewithal to indulge in several exotic pursuits, including aviation and yachting, but it was auto racing that really held his attention. Cunningham competed in a variety of cars before setting out to win the most prestigious sports car

Jaguar

The British marque is perhaps best known for its glorious successes at Le Mans in the 1950s, but Jaguars also have a rich heritage in the United States. Bob Tullius won many events with a variety of Jaguars, while West Coast racer Joe Huffaker provided a stiff rivalry to the Group 44 operation, especially in

SCCA competition.

Tullius was largely responsible for Jaguar's return to international sports car competition in 1984, with his tidy XJR-4, and subsequently Tom Walkinshaw Racing joined the fray with full factory support to win famously both at Le Mans and in the Rolex 24 Hours at Daytona.

Lola

The most prolific race car manufacturer of all, Lola Cars won the inaugural Can-Am in 1966 when Englishman John Surtees—the only man to secure world championships on both two and four wheels—claimed three races in his Chevy V8-powered T70.

Subsequent Can-Am challengers were not nearly so successful, until the series was resurrected in 1977 for Formula 5000 machinery clothed in all-enveloping bodywork, when Lola's T333-CS and its derivatives swept all before them.

The new T530 was equally dominant in 1980, especially in the hands of French Formula 1 driver Patrick Tambay. Lola also enjoyed success in IMSA as expatriate Englishman Brian Redman took Cooke-Woods Racing's T600 to the Camel GT title in 1980.

BRIGGS CUNNINGHAM *He took his cars to Le Mans and took the title home with him.*

MARCH *made cars for every motor sport at one time and the March Can-Am (above) won four times in 1981.*

March

Founded in 1969 by (now FIA president) Max Mosley, Alan Rees, Graham Coaker, and Robin Herd, March burst into the sport by producing cars for almost every category imaginable in 1970, including Formula 1 and Can-Am. Chris Amon took the 707 to a couple of fourth-place finishes but the car was never developed to its full potential.

March returned to the Can-Am with more success as Teo Fabi 11 years later, driving for Paul Newman, won four times and placed second in the standings. The company also entered the IMSA ranks, and later took the Camel GTP series in 1983 and '84. By then March had found a niche in Indy Car racing, which it dominated through the middle 1980s.

McLaren

Bruce McLaren established his own race car construction business while still driving for the factory Cooper team in Formula 1. His sights were initially set, however, on the 'big banger' sports racing category which was flourishing in the United States.

After first purchasing and totally refurbishing Roger Penske's famous Zerex Special Cooper in 1964, McLaren produced his first design, the Mark 1, later that year.

Subsequent McLarens went on to take the Can-Am series by storm. In all, and despite some fierce opposition, McLarens won 43 of the 71 races held between 1966 and '74, including a remarkable sequence of 23 straight between 1968 and '70.

'THE BRUCE AND DENNY SHOW' *1967–72 saw McLaren and Hulme dominate Can-Am.*

Porsche

The German marque has provided the backbone of IMSA (now SportsCar) competition since its inception. A wide variety of cars have been successful, with Peter Gregg and Al Holbert remaining as the two most successful drivers in IMSA history. Porsches have won the Daytona 24 Hours no fewer than 19 times and the Sebring 12 Hours on 17 occasions, including 13 in a row between 1976 and '88.

There were various developments of the Group 5 935, culminating in the bewinged 'Moby Dick' cars of the late '70s, and the famously reliable 962 which ruled the roost in Group C a decade later. In all, Porsche accounted for 286 overall and class wins in IMSA prior to the '97 season—plus 78 Trans-Am wins (second only to Chevrolet) and six championships.

PORSCHE POWER *Throughout IMSA history Porsche have been on top with cars like the 917 shown here.*

Riley & Scott

Veteran design engineer Bob Riley has worked on projects as diverse as the Saturn rocket, the Ford Taurus and Thunderbird sedans, and A.J. Foyt's Coyote Indy cars of the 1970s. Mark Scott, meanwhile, is an accomplished auto racing mechanic who spent time with several Formula 1 teams before moving to North America in 1984.

The pair first worked together in 1985, on McLaren North America's BMW GTP program, and five years' later set up in business together. Initially they produced generic Trans-Am cars, which proved extremely successful, before branching out into the IMSA WSC category. Wayne Taylor won the title in 1996 with Doyle Racing's Oldsmobile Aurora-powered R&S Mk.III.

Scarab

Soon after Lance Reventlow, heir to the Woolworth fortune, began racing in the mid-1950s, he decided the best way to win was to build his own cars. In 1957, Reventlow Automobiles Inc was born.

Reventlow first set his sights on the 1958 World Sports Car Championship, only to have his hopes scuppered when the FIA introduced a 3.0-liter engine limit, which immediately outlawed his Chevrolet V8 engine. The prototype Scarab nevertheless became the first American car to win a major international race in 40 years when Reventlow triumphed at Nassau during the Bahamas Speed Week.

The cars reaped tremendous success in the US, but neither they nor a subsequent Formula 1 entry achieved international recognition to match their looks before RAI was wound up in 1963.

Shadow

When Don Nicholls first unveiled his Advanced Vehicles Systems Shadow Mk.1 Can-Am challenger in 1970, most onlookers were quite unprepared for what lay before them. In common with most of its rivals, the Trevor Harris design was powered by a Chevrolet V8, but there the similarity ended. The car was absurdly small compared to the 'conventional' McLarens and Lolas. It resembled a go-kart rather than a car—but with a massive engine in the rear!

The subsequent Shadows were a lot more conventional and (whisper it) a lot more competitive. In 1974, the swan-song of the 'real' Can-Am, Briton Jackie Oliver (later to found the Arrows marque in F1) won four out of five races to claim a deserved championship in the DN4.

Shelby

Former chicken farmer Carroll Shelby first raced an MG TC in 1952, aged 29, and soon established an enviable reputation both in closed and open wheel cars. He raced for Aston Martin, Ferrari and Jaguar before retiring in 1960, due to a heart ailment. Instead, he set his sights on beating the best as a constructor.

Shelby creations including the Cobra, based on a British AC chassis and employing a 4.7-liter Ford V8 motor, which claimed the 1965 FIA Manufacturers' GT title (ahead of Ferrari); and the sports-racing 'King Cobras'—modified Coopers fitted with trusty Ford V8s. Shelby also masterminded the Ford GT40 program which yielded four straight Le Mans victories between 1966 and '69. Glorious days!

THE TRACKS

Daytona International Speedway

The Daytona Beach area has been a hotbed of auto racing activity since 1903, when Ransom E. Olds (later of Oldsmobile fame) put his 'Pirate' car through its paces on the hard-packed sand.

Regular speed trials were held until the mid-1930s, while stock car races continued on the beach until 1958, when NASCAR founder Bill France relocated the festivities to his new Daytona International Speedway course.

Daytona has hosted major international sports car races since 1962. Dan Gurney won the first three-hour event in a Lotus 19. The first 24-hour race was held in 1966. Ken Miles and Lloyd Ruby emerged victorious in a Ford GT Mk.II, averaging 108.020 mph on the combined oval/road course.

MIDNIGHT RUN *Racing through the dark at Daytona has taken place since 1966 and the first 24-hour race.*

Laguna Seca Raceway

Set among the sandy hills overlooking the Monterey Bay, Laguna Seca Raceway offers sensational viewing for spectators and a real challenge for the drivers. The famed 'Corkscrew' turn is among the most notorious within the sport, representing a hard left turn after which the road plunges steeply downhill, then sweeps once again to the right.

The track is run by a non-profit organization, SCRAMP (Sports Car Racing Association of the Monterey Peninsula), and was constructed on a vacant portion of the (now disused) Fort Ord Army base in 1957 after a well-established road race in nearby Pebble Beach (which continues to host a world-renowned *concours d'elegance* each year) outgrew its environment.

Riverside International Raceway

Richie Ginther and Ricardo Rodriguez, both of whom later raced in Formula 1, were among the winners at the inaugural Riverside event on September 21, 1957. The following year, the Los Angeles Times-Mirror sponsored a major sports car race which saw a titanic struggle between eventual winner Chuck Daigh (Scarab-Chevrolet) and Phil Hill (Ferrari 412MI).

Riverside hosted its first and only US Grand Prix in 1960, when Stirling Moss triumphed at the wheel of Rob Walker's Lotus-Climax 18. Thanksgiving weekend in 1964 saw the first-ever SCCA American Road Race of Champions, forerunner of the Valvoline Runoffs, which later became a regular stop on the Can-Am schedule. Sadly, due to encroaching suburbia, the track closed in 1988.

MIXED BLESSINGS *Pain for the drivers and pleasure for the spectators, Laguna Seca features the infamous 'corkscrew' turn.*

RIVERSIDE *A regular Can-Am stop and a motor sport favorite, this track sadly closed in 1988.*

Road America

Set among rolling hills and wooded pastures in rural Wisconsin, Road America has been a home to sports car racing for over 40 years. The track was built on land acquired by a group of wealthy racers after their former stomping ground, around the streets of nearby Elkhart Lake, a sleepy resort village, drew criticism from the local inhabitants.

Elkhart Lake's long straights are interspersed with tight corners and dramatic elevation changes to provide one of the classic venues in North America. The facility has been upgraded in recent years but its character remains undiminished.

The four-mile course has hosted many Can-Am and IMSA events, and has witnessed a Trans-Am event every year since 1970. The successful annual Chicago Historics event is another staple.

Sebring International Raceway

Alec Ulmann is responsible for establishing this former military training base as the scene for one of the world's premier endurance events. Indeed, the Sam Collier 6 Hour Memorial, held December 31, 1950, was the first sports car endurance race ever held in the US.

Sebring Raceway hosted its first 12-hour race in 1952, won by the Frazer-Nash of Harry Gray and Larry Kulok, and the following year it marked the first round of the fledgling FIA World Sports Car Championship.

Sebring also hosted the first ever US Grand Prix in December 1959, with Bruce McLaren emerging as the youngest winner in F1 history.

The layout has been much altered over the years, but the current configuration still provides a true test of man and machine over the bumpy former runways and link roads.

Watkins Glen

Still regarded as the spiritual home of Formula 1 in the US, despite the fact it has not hosted a Grand Prix since 1980, Watkins Glen has been a bastion for sports car racing ever since Cameron Argetsinger first opened the twisting, undulating permanent road course in 1956.

Prior to that, Watkins Glen had gained fame in 1948 by playing host to the first major SCCA event, which was held on a 6.6-mile course made entirely of public roads in and around the small town situated at the southern end of Seneca Lake in upstate New York.

STATISTICS

U.S. ROAD RACING CHAMPIONSHIPS

1963 Bob Holbert (Porsche R61/King Cobra-Ford)
1964 Jim Hall (Chaparral 2)
1965 George Follmer (Lola-Porsche 23)
1966 Chuck Parsons
(Genie Mk.10/McLaren-Chevrolet M1B)
1967 Mark Donohue (Lola-Chevrolet T70)
1968 Mark Donohue (McLaren-Chevrolet M6B)

CANADIAN-AMERICAN CHALLENGE CUP

1966 John Surtees (Lola-Chevrolet T70)
1967 Bruce McLaren (McLaren-Chevrolet M6A)
1968 Denis Hulme (McLaren-Chevrolet M8A)
1969 Bruce McLaren (McLaren-Chevrolet M8B)
1970 Denis Hulme (McLaren-Chevrolet M8D)
1971 Peter Revson (McLaren-Chevrolet M8F)
1972 George Follmer (Porsche 917/10K)
1973 Mark Donohue (Porsche 917/30K)
1974 Jackie Oliver (Shadow-Chevrolet DN4)
1977 Patrick Tambay (Lola-Chevrolet T333-CS)
1978 Alan Jones (Lola-Chevrolet T333-CS)
1979 Jacky Ickx (Lola-Chevrolet T333-CS)
U2L—Tim Evans (Lola-Ford T290)
1980 Patrick Tambay (Lola-Chevrolet T530)
U2L—Gary Gove (Ralt-Hart RT-2)
1981 Geoff Brabham
(Lola-Chevrolet T530/VDS-Chevrolet 001)
U2L—Jim Trueman (Ralt-Hart RT-2)
1982 Al Unser Jr (Frissbee-Chevrolet GR-3)
U2L—Bertil Roos (Marguey-Hart)
1983 Jacques Villeneuve (Frissbee-Chevrolet GR-3)
U2L—Bertil Roos (Scandia-Hart B3)
1984 Michael Roe (VDS-Chevrolet 002/004)
U2L—Kim Campbell (March-BMW 832)
1985 Rick Miaskiewicz (Frissbee-Chevrolet)
U2L—Dr Lou Sell (March-BMW 832)
1986 Horst Kroll (Frissbee-Chevrolet KRE)

Note: U2L = Under 2.0 Liter class

SCCA TRANS-AMERICAN SEDAN CHAMPIONSHIP

1966 *Horst Kweck/Gaston Andrey
(Alfa Romeo GTA)
1967 *Jerry Titus (Ford Mustang)
1968 *Mark Donohue (Chevrolet Camaro)
1969 *Mark Donohue (Chevrolet Camaro)
1970 *Parnelli Jones (Ford Mustang)
1971 Mark Donohue (AMC Javelin)
1972 George Follmer (AMC Javelin)
1973 Peter Gregg (Porsche Carrera)
1974 Peter Gregg (Porsche Carrera)
1975 John Greenwood (Chevrolet Corvette)
1976 George Follmer (Porsche 934)
II—Jocko Maggiacomo (AMC Javelin)
1977 Bob Tullius (Jaguar XJ-S)
II—Ludwig Heimrath Sr. (Porsche 934)
1978 Bob Tullius (Jaguar XJ-S)
II—Greg Pickett (Chevrolet Corvette)
1979 Gene Bothello (Chevrolet Corvette)
II—John Paul Sr (Porsche 935)
1980 John Bauer (Porsche 911SC)
1981 Eppie Wietzes (Chevrolet Corvette)
1982 Elliott Forbes-Robinson (Pontiac Trans Am)
1983 David Hobbs (Chevrolet Camaro)
1984 Tom Gloy (Lincoln-Mercury Capri)
1985 Wally Dallenbach Jr (Lincoln-Mercury Capri)
1986 Wally Dallenbach Jr (Chevrolet Camaro)
1987 Scott Pruett (Lincoln-Mercury XR4Ti)
1988 Hurley Haywood (Audi 200 Turbo Quattro)
1989 Dorsey Schroeder (Ford Mustang)
1990 Tom Kendall (Chevrolet Beretta)
1991 Scott Sharp (Chevrolet Camaro)
1992 Jack Baldwin (Chevrolet Camaro)
1993 Scott Sharp (Chevrolet Camaro)
1994 Scott Pruett (Chevrolet Camaro)
1995 Tom Kendall (Ford Mustang Cobra)
1996 Tom Kendall (Ford Mustang Cobra)

* = The Drivers' Championship was not officially instituted until 1971
II = Category II

IMSA GT CHAMPIONSHIP

1971 GT—David Heinz (Chevrolet Corvette)
GTU—Peter Gregg (Porsche 914/6)
1972 GT—Phil Currin (Chevrolet Corvette)
GTU—Hurley Haywood (Porsche 911S)
1973 GT—Peter Gregg (Porsche Carrera)
GTU—Bob Bergstrom (Porsche 911S)
1974 GT—Peter Gregg (Porsche Carrera)
GTU—Walt Maas (Porsche 911S)
1975 GT—Peter Gregg (Porsche Carrera)
GTU—Bob Sharp (Datsun Z)
1976 AAGT—Al Holbert (Porsche Carrera/Chevrolet Monza)
GTU—Brad Frisselle (Datsun Z)
1977 AAGT—Al Holbert (Chevrolet Monza)
GTU—Walt Maas (Porsche 911S)
1978 GTX—Peter Gregg (Porsche 935 Turbo)
GTO—David Cowart (Porsche Carrera)
GTU—Dave White (Porsche 911S)
1979 GTX—Peter Gregg (Porsche 935 Turbo)
GTO—Howard Meister (Porsche Carrera)
GTU—Don Devendorf (Datsun 280Z)
1980 GTX—John Fitzpatrick (Porsche 935 Turbo)
GTO—Luiz Mendez (Porsche Carrera)
GTU—Walt Bohren (Mazda RX-7)
1981 GTP—Brian Redman (Porsche 935/Lola-Chevrolet T600)
GTO—David Cowart (BMW M1)
GTU—Lee Mueller (Mazda RX-7)
1982 GTP—John Paul Jr (Porsche 935/Lola-Chevrolet T600)
GTO—Don Devendorf (Datsun ZX Turbo)
GTU—Jim Downing (Mazda RX-7)
1983 GTP—Al Holbert (March-Chevrolet/Porsche 83G)
GTO—Wayne Baker (Porsche 934)
GTU—Roger Mandeville (Mazda RX-7)
1984 GTP—Randy Lanier (March-Chevrolet 84G)
GTO—Roger Mandeville (Mazda RX-7)
GTU—Jack Baldwin (Mazda RX-7)
1985 GTP—Al Holbert (Porsche 962)
Lights—Jim Downing (Argo-Mazda JM16)
GTO—John Jones (Ford Mustang)
GTU—Jack Baldwin (Mazda RX-7)
1986 GTP—Al Holbert (Porsche 962)
Lights—Jim Downing (Argo-Mazda JM19)
GTO—Scott Pruett (Ford Mustang)
GTU—Tom Kendall (Mazda RX-7)

1987 GTP—Chip Robinson (Porsche 962)
Lights—Jim Downing (Argo-Mazda JM19)
GTO—Chris Cord (Toyota Celica Turbo)
GTU—Tom Kendall (Mazda RX-7)
1988 GTP—Geoff Brabham (Nissan GTP ZX-Turbo)
Lights—Tom Hessert Jr (Tiga/Chevrolet/Buick GT286)
GTO—Scott Pruett (Lincoln-Mercury XR4Ti)
GTU—Tom Kendall (Chevrolet Beretta GTU)
1989 GTP—Geoff Brabham (Nissan GTP ZX-Turbo)
Lights—Scott Schubot (Spice-Buick SE89P)
GTO—Pete Halsmer (Mercury Cougar XR-7)
GTU—Bob Leitzinger (Nissan 240SX)
1990 GTP—Geoff Brabham
(Nissan GTP ZX-Turbo/NPT90)
Lights—Tomas Lopez (Spice-Buick SE88/90P)
GTO—Dorsey Schroeder (Mercury Cougar XR-7)
AAC—Clay Young (Pontiac Firebird/Chevrolet Beretta)
GTU—Lance Stewart (Mazda MX-6)
1991 GTP—Geoff Brabham (Nissan R90C/NPT90-91)
Lights—Parker Johnstone (Spice-Acura SE90P)
GTO—Pete Halsmer (Mazda RX-7)
AAC—Dick Greer (Chevrolet Camaro)
GTU—John Fergus (Dodge Daytona)
1992 GTP—Juan Fangio II (Eagle-Toyota Mk.III)
Lights—Parker Johnstone (Spice-Acura SE91P)
GTS—Steve Millen (Nissan 300ZX Turbo)
GTO—Irv Hoerr (Oldsmobile Cutlass)
GTU—David Loring (Nissan 240SX)
1993 GTP—Juan Fangio II (Eagle-Toyota Mk.III)
Lights—Parker Johnstone (Spice-Acura SE92P)
GTS—Tom Kendall (Ford Mustang)
GTO—Charles Morgan (Oldsmobile Cutlass)
GTU—Butch Leitzinger (Nissan 240SX)
1994 WSC—Wayne Taylor (Kudzu-Mazda DG-3)
GTS—Steve Millen (Nissan 300ZX Turbo)
GTO—Joe Pezza (Oldsmobile Cutlass)
GTU—Jim Pace (Porsche 911/Nissan 240SX)
1995 WSC—Fermin Velez (Ferrari 333SP)
GTS-1—Irv Hoerr (Oldsmobile Cutlass)
GTS-2—Jorge Trejos (Porsche 911 RSR)
1996 WSC—Wayne Taylor (R&S-Oldsmobile Mk.III)
GTS-1—Irv Hoerr (Oldsmobile Aurora)
GTS-2—Larry Schumacher (Porsche 911)

DIRT TRACK

Once a stepping stone toward the Indianapolis 500, dirt tracking now stands on its own with America's other forms of big-time racing.

Since the days of barnstorming race car drivers early this century, dirt track racing in the United States has undergone ebbs and flows in popularity. Many of the historic tracks those racers visited still exist; others have long since been replaced by homes or strip malls. But new tracks are under construction in places like Los Angeles and Las Vegas, as dirt track racing regains its popularity and sets out to broaden its audience.

The genre exists in virtually every corner of the States, but it remains most popular in rural areas of the Midwest. The hotbed of major league dirt racing—in which sprint cars are most popular—is centered loosely from western Pennsylvania through Ohio, Indiana, Illinois, and into Iowa, home of the biggest dirt sprint car race, the Knoxville Nationals. Late model racing—now a highly modified version of stock cars—is popular in the Midwest and South, and small, rural tracks across the country are rife with weekend events for various forms of stock racing.

The premier dirt series—the World of Outlaws sprint car series—ranked fifth in total US attendance in 1996, drawing nearly 1.6 million fans. That trails only the NASCAR Winston Cup and Busch Grand National stock cars, CART Indy cars, and NHRA drag racing.

Two other touring series are popular in the Midwest, Northeast, and portions of the South: the United States Auto Club (USAC) and the All Star Circuit of Champions. USAC, the sanctioning body behind the Indy 500, features tours for three divisions: Silver Crown (what used to be known as champ or big cars), a larger, more powerful open wheel, sprint-type car; non-winged sprint cars; and midgets, a small, four-cylinder version of the sprint car. All three series run on dirt and paved tracks, dominated by Kenny Irwin Jr, Billy Boat, Doug Kalitta, and Jimmy Sills.

The All Star Circuit of Champions, like the World of Outlaws, is strictly a dirt track series for winged sprint cars. Big name All Star Circuit drivers include Dale Blaney, Frankie Kerr, and Kenny Jacobs, while leading Outlaws are Steve Kinser, Mark Kinser, Sammy Swindell, Jeff Swindell, Jac Haudenschild, Dave Blaney and Andy Hillenburg.

The most famous American dirt track is Knoxville Raceway, a half-mile oval located in a town of 8,000 in the middle of Iowa's rich cornfields. The track began as a diversion for county fairgoers in the 1940s. It now seats 23,000 fans, features suites towering over the second turn, and hosts the most influential and richest sprint car race in the world: the Knoxville Nationals.

The Nationals, a four-day event each August which pays $100,000 to the winner, began in 1960 as a race for supermodifieds, which evolved into sprint cars by the late 1960s. The event has grown so quickly in recent years that it threatens to outgrow the facility. For its third consecutive televised race in summer 1997, Knoxville added more suites, stretching atop the main grandstand from the fourth to the first turn.

Knoxville's chief rival is Eldora Speedway in Rossburg, Ohio, which began as a diversion for a bandleader. Earl Baltes, the track's owner and promoter, built a dirt track next to his country ballroom. A few decades later, it's the site of two $100,000 prize sprint car races: the King's Royal and The Big One.

While the two most influential dirt tracks lie on either side of Indiana, the Hoosier state is the undisputed capital of dirt tracks and sprint cars. Famous tracks lie in small Indiana towns like Winchester, Salem, and Terre Haute. From here, drivers hope to reach the Indianapolis 500.

Even today, many of the top stars in racing hail from Indiana: NASCAR's Jeff Gordon, the Indy Racing League's Tony Stewart and sprint car racing's famous Kinser family are among them. Dirt tracking maintains its grassroots bond, producing stars in other forms of racing while standing on its own popularity.

DIRT FEVER *Dirt Tracks are being built all over America now and racers like Gary Bettenhausen are pulling in the crowds.*

THE HISTORY

LEGEND *Barney Oldfield has a tire change which appears to be taking a little longer than those of today.*

n the US, dirt racing began almost as soon as the first automobiles were built. It remained an exclusive form of racing until the 1920s and '30s, when board and brick tracks were laid. Pavement became the preferred surface, but dirt tracks still gave man and machine the toughest test. Legendary drivers like Barney Oldfield and Eddie Rickenbacker in the 1910s and '20s, Rex Mays in the 1930s and '40s, and A.J. Foyt and Mario Andretti in the '50s and '60s honed their skills on dirt, then made their names on wood, brick, cinder, and concrete tracks.

Surprisingly, in the latter part of this century, when unpaved roads exist only in the most rural parts of the country, dirt track racing thrives. Not surprisingly, it thrives in those same rural areas, on quarter-, half-, and even full mile tracks. It's a different scene, drawing tens of thousands of fans, some sitting in enclosed suites to watch major races. Television brings the largest dirt track events into the homes of millions of Americans. Nearly all dirt races are held at night, and tracks are groomed and watered carefully; the surfaces become so hard and smooth that they resemble pavement, providing maximum traction and wearing heavily on tires.

In many ways, however, racing on dirt remains as simple as it was in the days of Oldfield and Rickenbacker. Except for stock car races at small tracks and some larger late model events, dirt cars are generally open-wheel machines—the most popular being the sprint car.

The modern sprint car evolved from a combination of the super-modified and champ car of the 1950s. Its present form isn't far removed from what Mays drove in his AAA days or what Foyt and Andretti drove in USAC competition—a small, single-seat, front-engine roadster with a fuel tank in the tail.

The differences, on the other hand, are radical. The modern sprinter can produce nearly 700 horsepower and reach speeds of more than 130 mph along the straightaways of half-mile tracks. A huge wing over the rollcage became mandatory for some sanctioning bodies in the late 1970s and early '80s, designed to prevent cars flipping over. And the tires are nothing like the bicycle-like tubes of the early days. Nearly two feet wide, the right rear tire often has little air, providing even more grip.

As the sport approaches its second century, dirt track racing has reverted to its roots. When Oldfield and Rickenbacker drove, dirt tracks were the only way to go. Now, drivers don't necessarily use dirt tracks to reach another form of racing; when they get to the highest levels on dirt, they've made it.

BOBBY UNSER *Number 5, seen here leading from Jim McElreath during the USAC 100 Miller in 1966.*

THE DRIVERS

Guy Forbrook

If you were an opponent on a dirt track, Guy Forbrook would want you to fear him before the race, then chat afterward. He has a spell over people, the power to make them do things they'd never consider without the push of his little-boy grin and the knowledge of what's behind it.

Forbrook is one of the best sprint car owners and mechanics in the US. He's the most successful owner in the history of the famous Knoxville Raceway in Iowa, and has had victories from New York to California, against the World of Outlaws, the All Star Circuit of Champions, and the locals.

"I admire him," said Doug Wolfgang, who raced with Forbrook and Forbrook's father, Dick. "I would have admired him no matter what, but I admire him more now than I did when he first came back because I hadn't been hurt yet. He had a devastating injury, and mine was just a burn. Even though he's a little smart-ass and a little cocky, he's still one of my heroes. Anybody who can do what he did deserves the applause."

For a brief time in 1986, Forbrook wasn't big on himself. A traffic accident left a lightning-fast, 24-year-old

GUY FORBROOK *A tireless worker driven by a desire to win and win and win again.*

sprint car driver lying motionless in University of Minnesota hospitals in Minneapolis. He had no movement from the waist down, and it wasn't going to return. He wasn't sure what he would do or where he would turn. For once, the fearless racer was afraid.

"I was scared as hell," Forbrook admitted. "I had no clue what the hell I was going to do. I never had a clue this would happen the way it did or how good it was going to go or anything. I was just lucky, I guess. It happened. I met with the right people and it took off."

The right people, in this case, were Al Cole and Danny Lasoski. Cole supplied the money to get Forbrook's car back on the track, and Lasoski got behind the wheel. Together, they turned the purple No.5 into a winning machine across the Midwest. In their first summer together (1989), they shocked the Outlaws by stealing a feature race in Oklahoma City. By 1992, they were at their peak, finishing second to Steve Kinser in the Knoxville Nationals. When they venture outside their home tracks, Knoxville and Huset's Speedway near Sioux Falls, South Dakota, they run competitively with anyone—and often outrun them.

"That race car is probably what saved him," said Terry McCarl, who drove Forbrook's car briefly while Lasoski took another ride in 1994. "It's what's given him his great optimism. I wouldn't say it's given him something to live for, but it's given him a goal he can work toward."

The goal keeps him moving. Forbrook gets around a race track better than his counterparts. He routinely rides his four-wheeler from one end of the infield to the other, constantly checking the track and his car's response to it.

"I don't think he knows he's in a wheelchair," McCarl said. "Lasoski and I ran into each other one night up at Huset's. I rammed Danny in the back, and Guy didn't see the humor in that. He came down and told me he was going to kick my butt. That was before I drove for him, of course."

He isn't the average car owner. While some drive and others watch, Forbrook works. He's often out of the chair, covered in dirt, wrenching

away under the car. He doesn't just direct the work, he does the work.

"It's desire," he said. "Just desire. That's the bottom line, to win at any cost, anywhere. The way I see it, when you strap the belts on, you have no friends. If you have a friend, you're not going to cut it—not with the World of Outlaws. You might win at local shows, but if you're not willing to lay it on the line, you're not going to get it done."

As far as he's concerned, his life has nothing to do with the chair. The chair and the four-wheeler are only tools, no different than a floor jack or impact wrench. McCarl: "When you look at Guy, you don't picture him as being any different than anybody else. That's the way we should look at people in wheelchairs or with any other kind of handicap, but it's hard to do.

"But truly, with Guy Forbrook, it's his personality. It's what he does. I'm sure in his heart he's had to deal with it, but he'd never let that out. He doesn't have a problem with it, so you don't."

Jac Haudenschild

Things didn't go so well for Jac Haudenschild in 1996. He lost his health, he lost racing, and he lost his sponsor. Like a dream, it all came back to him in 1997—better than ever.

In August 1996, Haudenschild sustained a back injury when his sprint car flipped during a World of Outlaws race at West Lebanon, New York, forcing him to miss the Knoxville Nationals and the rest of the season. While healing, Haudenschild's plan to return took another spill: his sponsor, Pennzoil, dropped him.

Within a month, though, Pennzoil changed its corporate mind. Not only did it return to Haudenschild's team, they decided to sponsor the entire series. The World of Outlaws is now the Pennzoil World of Outlaws.

In 1997, Haudenschild was off to his best start with the Outlaws. He's also still wondering exactly what happened during the off-season.

"We really don't know how [Pennzoil] came back," Haudenschild said. "My car owner, Jack Elden, wrote them a letter and asked them why they dropped us. They didn't really say anything. A few weeks later, they called back and came back with us. We didn't really know what was going on."

Guy Forbrook didn't know what was going on, either. Shortly after last season ended, he was hired to manage Elden's team.

Forbrook celebrated his seventh track championship in the last eight years at Knoxville Raceway by selling his storied No.5 sprint car. He also sold his truck, his trailer… everything but five motors… when the telephone rang in November with the bad news.

"It was sort of tough, especially after I'd agreed to do all of this stuff and I'd let go of my own team," Forbrook said. "And my own team had been very successful at what we were doing. I was frustrated that I'd let everything go and then Pennzoil decided to quit, and there I sat. But you just get up and go

after it the next day."

Elden went after it, too, but in a different way. His letter to Pennzoil was followed by phone calls to the company's lawyers, more faxes, more phone calls, and the unexpected: letters from race fans angered by the decision. "A large portion of it had to do with the fans," Elden said. "[Pennzoil] got a very adverse reaction from the fans with respect to the fact that they weren't going to renew for next year.

"I contacted their legal counsel, and we discussed some issues, and that was it. I explained my position, and what the facts were, and made sure they understood what commitments had been made to us."

Pennzoil's fumble and recovery was a combination of misunderstandings and new faces. Rumor had it that Elden was going to retire. Wrong, he said. And, after a personnel shakeup at Pennzoil, Elden wasn't sure who was in charge. Eventually, though, everything was sorted out.

JAC HAUDENSCHILD *Who made his comeback in 1997.*

"We got a fairly quick response after we got our things together. There'd been such a change down there, the only person I could talk to was the legal counsel. All the people we'd worked with over the years were gone. It didn't surprise me that they came back to the team, because I think we were basically right."

With a motor Forbrook used in the No.5 car when Danny Lasoski drove it the previous season, Haudenschild is running up front with the Outlaws. "We've got good equipment again," Forbrook said. "I took the motor from my car from last year and dropped it in their car for this year. I really didn't have to do any chasing; I just sold it to them"

As a result, Haudenschild got a strong start to a season that cannot possibly be worse than the previous one. "Last year was a disaster," he conceded. "From hurting my back and having a plate taken out of my arm, I never really was 100 per cent. But this year, we started out good. Guy's got the car running good, and the motors are good. Everything's quick. It doesn't look like we'll have any trouble running with them this year."

If you listen to Forbrook, the No.22 won't have any trouble running ahead of them: "I've got a bunch of new engine stuff in the works. We got started so late that I kind of had everything on the back burner. If we can stay in the top two in points all the way through June, I really think I can make these guys pay hell at the end of the year."

For four weeks in November, the outlook wasn't nearly as optimistic. During their time without a sponsor, Haudenschild, Forbrook, and Elden decided to run with the Outlaws anyway. It wasn't a promising proposition: 70 events, 100 dates, 44 tracks and 23 states. On two-thirds of the previous year's budget. Without Forbrook's equipment.

"Guy and I were working on a program to stay in racing. He was going to do certain things, and I would do certain things to help fund the team," Elden explained. We were going to put in everything we could, and he was going to put in everything he could, then we'd be sort of co-owners."

Then Pennzoil called. Upon further review, they were coming back. The TV numbers were strong, the exposure wide, the fans loyal, the price right.

Haudenschild didn't need a marketing degree to come to that conclusion. "We race a hundred races a year, up and down the road. I don't see where you could get any better advertisement in any kind of racing. Just the amount of races we run alone makes it worth it for the sponsors. At the different tracks each night, we see the people who change their own oil."

Those same people write a mean letter, too.

Kenny Irwin

By anyone else's standards, Kenny Irwin Jr enjoyed a prosperous season in 1996. He took the lead in both the USAC Silver Crown and national midget series at about the same time

KENNY IRWIN *Seen here winning the USAC Midget at Winchester Speedway in Indiana.*

early in the summer. He led the midget points to the finish, but lost the Silver Crown title in the final turn on the final lap of the final race.

"It's great to finish second, I guess, but when you run so good all year and don't win, it's tough," Irwin said. "I probably wanted that championship more than the midget deal, just because it's a little more prestigious. It's just a big deal."

Irwin needed to finish sixth or better in the Silver Crown season finale at Del Mar, California, to win the season title. While running fourth on the final lap, a tire was cut on Irwin's Chevy-powered Beast. He crashed, finished 11th, and Jimmy Sills claimed the season title by winning the race.

"A lot of people see that I had a real good year, but I see that I had a lot more disappointments than I've had in the past," Irwin said. "That's because you run good and you just come up short. You have a lot more hope for yourself than other people do. They think running second is pretty good. I don't." Perhaps feeling the pressure of Tony Stewart's sprint midget champ sweep in 1995, Irwin walked from his wrecked car at Del Mar to the parking lot and drove away.

"We ran good all year, but to me, there were more disappointments than high points. Winning the champ car race at Indianapolis Raceway Park was a real big race this year. It's so hard just to win a champ car race, not to mention trying to put the championship and everything with it."

Instead, the championship and everything with it went to Sills, whose Mopar-powered car began creeping up on Irwin and early leader Mike Bliss after a victory in the fourth race of the year at Richmond. By the time the series reached Sacramento, Sills led the points race. But it wasn't until long after he drove past Irwin's wrecked car at Del Mar that Sills knew he'd won the championship.

"I didn't even see Kenny sitting there in the corner," Sills said. "I was just excited because we'd won the race. I drove right by him. He was up in the shadows where you couldn't see him. I pulled up to the front straightaway and thought, 'I wonder where

Kenny finished.' Then I just forgot about it—hey, we'd won the race.

"Then they came down and said, 'Hey, Kenny didn't make it past the checkered flag.' I didn't want to believe it until they announced it."

Karl Kinser

Shortly after winning the 1996 Knoxville Nationals for the first time, Mark Kinser said something unusual: "To be honest, I would have

liked to have done this on my own, back when I was doing my own deal without Dad. That doesn't mean I'm not happy with this, it just means I'd like to have proved that I was good enough to do it without him."

A more sincere statement of flattery will probably never be uttered. In essence, Kinser was telling everyone else what the world of sprint car racing already knew: His father, Karl Kinser, owns the game. If you can win without him preparing your car, you're something special.

As a car owner and crew chief, Karl Kinser has won the World of Outlaws' title 15 times in the series'

19 years of existence. The first 14 titles were with cousin Steve Kinser at the wheel. This one, however, was with Mark. "I think my record speaks for itself," Karl said. "I've never had a loser driving my car. I think a little bit of that can be attributed to myself." Perhaps more than just a little.

Karl Kinser is to sprint car racing what the Wright brothers were to the airplane, and the sprint car is to present day racing what their first plane was to the modern airliner. There are no computers, no telemetry, only minor aerodynamics. The task Karl Kinser and his peers face is to deliver between 600 and 700 horsepower to

KARL KINSER *Owner and mechanic on 15 championships; 14 with his cousin and one with his son.*

the ground as efficiently as possible.

No one is more efficient than Kark Kinser. From a modest shop behind his log home in Oolitic, Indiana, have come some of the fastest sprint cars of the past 20 years. He's virtually reinvented the machine: The slider clutch, plastic fuel cell, hydraulic wing slider, and his use of titanium and aluminum parts have revolutionized sprint cars. Most of these inventions were by-products of his compulsions.

"I'll be in the shop until 3 or 4 in the morning, tinkering around with something I wanted to try, while the other guy was lying at home watching football or was out at the bar," Kinser said. "That's how I gained a lot of my experience.

"You can name anybody, and no matter how many hours he's said he's worked on a race car, I can double it. I don't care who you're talking about—Jesus Christ or anybody else you can name. A lot of my knowledge comes from that tinkering, and it's been no easy task. If I win a race, I think I've deserved it. If I win 20 in a row, I think I've deserved them."

Mark Kinser

Mark Kinser knew he wasn't going to repeat as World of Outlaws champion before the 1997 season began. He missed two Outlaws races early in the season while attempting to qualify for a NASCAR SuperTruck race at Phoenix International Raceway. By missing the races, he lost enough points to plummet from first to 16th and lost any chance he had to win the 1997 Outlaws title.

"When I committed to the truck series earlier in the year, I had a feeling it would come to a point where we would either be leading the points or be up close to the front," Kinser said. "I knew the dilemma was going to happen before it ever did. I was prepared for it, anyway."

Karl Kinser, Mark's father and car owner, put Mark's cousin, Kelly, in the No.5 car for the two races. Kelly Kinser won at West Plains (Missouri) Motor Speedway, then finished second at Missouri International Raceway Park in Benton. Meanwhile, another cousin, Steve, took over the Outlaws' points lead.

"It don't really bother me none," Karl Kinser said of Mark's decision to try truck racing. "If you're ever going to try anything different or race for bigger purses, you've got to venture out sometime. Any time you do it, you're going to take a loss of income. It's like going to college. You pay tuition."

This one was costly, though. Not only did Mark Kinser lose his points lead with the Outlaws, he failed to qualify for the truck race, won by Jack Sprague. However, Kinser still led the Outlaws in prize money— $60,000—and Karl still led the car owners' points.

Mark Kinser expects to miss another 10–12 World of Outlaws races while pursuing the truck series.

"Once it's all said and done, he won't even be in the top 20," Karl Kinser predicted. "The way the Outlaw thing is done, they want you to run. They take enough points away from you that if you miss one race, you're not going to win the points thing. We knew that going in."

MARK KINSER *Commitment to NASCAR SuperTruck cost him any chance of the 1997 championship.*

Brian Tyler

Brian Tyler's big break didn't involve winning or luck. He became the first driver in 39 years to take the USAC national sprint car title without winning a feature race, and hopes to turn the championship into something else.

"I'd like to journey on, maybe to NASCAR trucks, or maybe even do some of this Indy Racing League," Tyler speculated. "It's just a matter of being in the right place at the right time and finding the right sponsors. It's opened things up a bunch for sprint car drivers. I think trucks have, too. Kenny Irwin and Andy Michner

just got truck rides, and those are guys I run with all summer long. That's a possibility for us now, too."

Winning a season championship without winning a race isn't as simple as it may sound. Tyler stayed close to the points lead, held early by Doug Kalitta, but during the three-race run of Indiana Speed Weeks, Kalitta encountered problems while Tyler ran well. At that point, he realized he could win the title.

"Doug had two or three bad nights," Tyler said. "That let me get ahead. It looked like it was possible then. At the beginning of the year, I was just hoping for a top five finish. I would have been happy with that."

As it turned out, he finished 176 points ahead of second-placed Kalitta. Brian Hayden took third, 51

points behind Kalitta, David Steele was fourth, Tim Cox fifth, and Bill Rose sixth. Jason McCord, Tyler's partner on Larry Contos' team, finished seventh.

A veteran of winged sprint shows in the upper Midwest—including the All Star Circuit of Champions and Sprints on Dirt—he'd never driven a non-winged sprinter before this season. "It was a big learning experience," he said. "You have to change your driving style a lot. At the first of the year, I was having problems with trying to drive it into the corners too deep. I wanted to run it like I still had a wing on it."

Tyler's relocation from Michigan to Contos' race shop in Anderson, Indiana, may have been the best

move he made all season: "I moved to be around the cars more than anything else. The guys treated me real well and were behind me 110 percent. They all kept telling me all year long that we were going to win the championship, but I kept telling them not to count it too early. They believed in me."

Doug Wolfgang

World of Outlaws officials weren't happy that Doug Wolfgang returned to race with their series, but they didn't try to stop him. Wolfgang raced with the Outlaws early in the

DOUG WOLFGANG *Pictured here previous to his horrific crash and the bitter legal battles that ensued.*

1997 season for the first time since he sued the sanctioning body and was awarded $1.2 million by a federal jury in August 1995. The verdict was appealed.

Wolfgang, who ranks third in total World of Outlaws victories behind Steve Kinser and Sammy Swindell, was severely burned in April 1992 when his car crashed and caught fire during practice at Lakeside Speedway in Kansas City. Unconscious from the impact, Wolfgang sat in his blazing vehicle for several minutes until fellow drivers rescued him. Instead of its own facilities, the World of Outlaws uses existing crews and equipment at the tracks it visits. As a result, drivers say, they see a wide variety of fire and rescue crews and equipment… from the professional to the incompetent.

Doug Wolfgang suffered life-threatening third- and fourth-degree burns over 35 percent of his body. He lost portions of his right foot and two fingers. He sued the Outlaws and the former owners and promoter at Lakeside, claiming gross negligence.

Ted Johnson, president of the World of Outlaws, didn't ban Wolfgang from racing when he tried to enter an event in 1997 at Knoxville Raceway. "He has to do what he feels is right within his mind," Johnson said. "If he's there, he'll be treated like any other racer. He's got to sign the release or he won't be allowed in the gates."

When the Outlaws visit Knoxville, the sanctioning body, not the track, has the final say on which drivers are allowed to race. Johnson could ban Wolfgang, track officials said, but doing so would run the risk of another lawsuit. The fact that Knoxville Raceway is operated by Marion County also influenced the decision to let him race.

"There is a possibility that if it were a privately-owned track, that individual could find some reason to keep Doug from racing, but it would be a gray area," explained Ralph Capitani, director of racing at Knoxville. "With a county-owned facility, it's virtually a cinch that there's no way they can keep him from racing—not without letting themselves open for another lawsuit."

Wolfgang hasn't raced with the World of Outlaws, a touring sprint car series based in Plano, Texas, since an aborted comeback attempt in 1994, after which he filed the suit which contended the Outlaws and Lakeside Speedway didn't provide adequate rescue crews and equipment.

Wolfgang said he wasn't concerned about Johnson's reaction to his return. "I'm concerned about the reaction from my friends and fans, and mostly, my peers. I'm more concerned with the reaction of the guys I raced with, guys like Steve [Kinser] and Sammy [Swindell] and [Dave] Blaney and Mark [Kinser]. It's not going to stop me from coming, but I could care less what Ted Johnson thinks of me."

The lawsuit has had an emotional and lasting impact on sprint car racing. Some people involved in the sport were angry with Wolfgang, others angry with Johnson.

"I've told Ted before that I don't know why he has a problem with what happened," said Karl Kinser, owner of a car driven by his son, Mark. "It wasn't Doug Wolfgang's fault. It was Ted's fault because he didn't have the stuff there. And he's pissed because he sued him? Why, the guy needs an attitude adjustment, doesn't he? Well, he got it."

The bitterness of the legal battle and the reaction to it still bother Wolfgang: "It took a lot of the love for the sport out of me, but I still love the sport. I just thought that at the time I got involved in the lawsuit, it was worth it to me, and it should have been done, and I needed to do it. I also knew going in that as soon as I filed that lawsuit, I was going to be a butthead nationwide, and I was.

"In my mind, I didn't falter. I knew what I was doing was for the betterment of the sport. It was my prerogative to do it, and I thought it was right. I wasn't going to feel wrong about it, so I stayed away from the race tracks for a couple of years."

BRIAN TYLER
The 1996 USAC Sprint Car champion is looking to convert to NASCAR or Indy car with this win under his belt.

IMCA

With a sport in a constant state of flux, the only thing more constant than change is the resistance to it. Nowhere is that more evident these days than in the breadbasket of dirt track racing.

The late model race car, long the staple of Saturday night shows in the Midwest, is in a state of upheaval. Car counts and morale are down, costs and tension high. Just when the future couldn't appear more bleak, along come major changes from a sanctioning body.

The International Motor Contest Association dropped a bomb on its late model class in October 1996 when it announced sweeping rule changes, including a 10.5-to-1 limit on compression ratio, spec heads, and a spec intake manifold. Several of IMCA's top drivers have left the sanctioning body to race in NASCAR events.

"It's a bad deal," said Jeff Aikey, who won the 1996 season championship of the IMCA's late model tour, the Deery Brothers Summer Series. "I've got $30,000 in engines now. For me to change, I'd have to build a whole new engine. Then I'd have new engines just sitting there."

IMCA officials say the changes are designed to cut costs; drivers say they'll have to spend more. Officials say they want to strengthen the class; drivers say the officials want to eliminate it. Officials say they're concerned about the good of the sport; drivers say they're only concerned about lining their pockets.

"Their concept is so far off and their touch with reality has missed the mark so far that it's almost impossible to describe people's feelings," said Jeff French, a past IMCA national late model champion and past winner of the Deery series. "The change, they claim, is going to cheapen the cost, but the racers feel that these associations that contend in the same sentence that they're going to save us money and slow the cars down are, in essence, making everyone spend more money to go slower."

While IMCA's modifieds have grown to the largest class of racing in America, its late models have suffered. Small Midwestern tracks struggle to keep late models in their weekly shows. Purses are low—IMCA-sanctioned weekly late model races rarely pay more than $500 to the winner, and participation has dwindled.

"It's a bad move, I really think it is," said Kathy Root, owner of IMCA. "It's something a lot of people aren't willing to do. They'll maintain the status quo until it's gone. That's not what we want to do. We want to initiate some growth."

BATTLE CARS *An early tussle for the lead at the Independence Motor Speedway.*

TEAMMATES *Gary Crawford (10) and Greg Hunter (7) flank Greg Kastli.*

BAD FEELING *IMCA's 1996 rule changes have led to drivers quitting the sport.*

Stock Car 1996

1996 WINSTON CUP SEASON'S STATISTICS

Races: 31.
Longest: 600 miles.
Shortest: 187 miles.
Race Laps: 9,648.
Race Miles: 11,747.33
Average Race: 311.2 Laps, 378.95 Miles.
Average Lap: 1.22 Miles.
Driver Attempting to Qualify: 87.
Drivers Starting Races: 67.
Pole Winners: 14.
Average Pole Winning Margin: 0.127 Second.
Average Starting Field: 40.6 Cars.
Average Number Running at Finish: 32.5
Average Number Finishing on Lead Lap: 12.5.
Average Number of Race Leaders: 9.5;
Average Lead Changes: 19.3.
Average Caution Flags per Race: 5.7.
Average Caution Laps: 34.2
Number of Race Winners: 11.
Average Winning Margin: 1.98 Seconds.
Most Races Led: Jeff Gordon 25.
Most Laps Led: Jeff Gordon 2,314.
Most Races Won: Jeff Gordon 10; Rusty Wallace 5.

JEFF GORDON *The driver who is dominating NASCAR in the 1990s.*

Indy Car 1996

CART

1979**	Rick Mears
1980	Johnny Rutherford
1981	Rick Mears
1982	Rick Mears
1983	Al Unser
1984	Mario Andretti
1985	Al Unser
1986	Bobby Rahal
1987	Bobby Rahal
1988	Danny Sullivan
1989	Emerson Fittipaldi
1990	Al Unser, Jr.
1991	Michael Andretti
1992	Bobby Rahal
1993	Nigel Mansell
1994	Al Unser, Jr.
1995	Jacques Villeneuve
1996	Jimmy Vasser

** The United States Auto Club and Championship Auto Racing Teams ran separate championships in 1979.

JIMMY VASSER *The jubilant 1996 CART winner.*

Drag Racing 1996

1996 NHRA WINSTON DRAG RACING SERIES RESULTS

WINTERNATIONALS—Pomona, Calif.
TOP FUEL	W: Blaine Johnson	R/U: Connie Kalitta
FUNNY CAR	W: Al Hofmann	R/U: John Force
PRO STOCK	W: Jim Yates	R/U: Billy Huff

ATSCO NATIONALS—Phoenix, Ariz.
TOP FUEL	W: Kenny Bernstein	R/U: Cory McClenathan
FUNNY CAR	W: John Force	R/U: Chuck Etchells
PRO STOCK	W: Jim Yates	R/U: Tom Martino

GATORNATIONALS—Gainesville, Fla.
TOP FUEL	W: Blaine Johnson	R/U: Scott Kalitta
FUNNY CAR	W: John Force	R/U: Chuck Etchells
PRO STOCK	W: Jim Yates	R/U: Steve Schmidt

SLICK 50 NATIONALS—Houston, Texas
TOP FUEL	W: Kenny Bernstein	R/U: Joe Amato
FUNNY CAR	W: John Force	R/U: Al Hofmann
PRO STOCK	W: Mike Edwards	R/U: Ray Franks
PRO STOCK BIKE	W: John Myers	R/U: Dave Schultz

FRAM NATIONALS—Atlanta, Ga.
TOP FUEL	W: Larry Dixon	R/U: Mike Dunn
FUNNY CAR	W: Tony Pedregon	R/U: John Force
PRO STOCK	W: Kurt Johnson	R/U: Jim Yates

PENNZOIL NATIONALS—Richmond, Va.
TOP FUEL	W: Shelly Anderson	R/U: Scott Kalitta
FUNNY CAR	W: John Force	R/U: Cruz Pedregon
PRO STOCK	W: Warren Johnson	R/U: Mike Edwards

MOPAR NATIONALS—Englishtown, N.J.
TOP FUEL	W: Joe Amato	R/U: Larry Dixon
FUNNY CAR	W: John Force	R/U: Gary Densham
PRO STOCK	W: Jim Yates	R/U: Warren Johnson

PONTIAC excitement NATIONALS—Columbus, Ohio
TOP FUEL	W: Cory McClenathan	R/U: Larry Dixon
FUNNY CAR	W: Chuck Etchells	R/U: Mark Oswald
PRO STOCK	W: Chuck Harris	R/U: Warren Johnson
PSB	W: Dave Schultz	R/U: Matt Hines

PENNZOIL NATIONALS—Memphis, Tenn.
TOP FUEL	W: Mike Dunn	R/U: Joe Amato
FUNNY CAR	W: John Force	R/U: Tony Pedregon
PRO STOCK	W: Warren Johnson	R/U: Jim Yates

WESTERN AUTO NATIONALS—Topeka, Kan.
TOP FUEL	W: Scott Kalitta	R/U: Kenny Bernstein
FUNNY CAR	W: John Force	R/U: Cruz Pedregon
PRO STOCK	W: Warren Johnson	R/U: Jim Yates

MILE-HIGH NATIONALS—Denver, Colo.
TOP FUEL	W: Eddie Hill	R/U: Blaine Johnson
FUNNY CAR	W: John Force	R/U: Chuck Etchells
PRO STOCK	W: Jim Yates	R/U: Stve Schmidt
PRO STOCK BIKE	W: Matt Hines	R/U: Dave Schultz

AUTOLITE NATIONALS—Sonoma, Calif.
TOP FUEL	W: Blaine Johnson	R/U: Kenny Bernstein
FUNNY CAR	W: Cruz Pedregon	R/U: John Force
PRO STOCK	W: Warren Johnson	R/U: Mike Edwards
SG	W: Ray Cordeiro	R/U: Jody Lang

NORTHWEST NATIONALS—Seattle, Wash,
TOP FUEL	W: Shelly Anderson	R/U: Mike Dunn
FUNNY CAR	W: John Force	R/U: Tony Pedregon
PRO STOCK	W: Mike Edwards	R/U: Kurt Johnson

CHAMPION AUTO STORES NATIONALS—Brainerd, Minn.
TOP FUEL	W: Kenny Bernstein	R/U: Eddie Hill
FUNNY CAR	W: John Force	R/U: Tony Pedregon
PRO STOCK	W: Warren Johnson	R/U: Steve Schmidt
PRO STOCK BIKE	W: Matt Hines	R/U: John Myers

U.S. NATIONALS—Indianapolis, Ind
TOP FUEL	W: Cory McClenathan	R/U: Tony Schumacher
FUNNY CAR	W: John Force	R/U: Al Hofmann
PRO STOCK	W: Kurt Johnson	R/U: Rickie Smith
PRO STOCK BIKE	W: John Myers	R/U: Matt Hines

KEYSTONE NATIONALS—Reading, Pa.
TOP FUEL	W: Kenny Bernstein	R/U: Connie Kalitta
FUNNY CAR	W: Jeff Arend	R/U: Tony Pedregon
PRO STOCK	W: Jim Yates	R/U: Warren Johnson
PRO STOCK BIKE	W: Angelle Seeling	R/U: Dave Schultz

SEARS CRAFTSMAN NATIONALS—Topeka, Kan.
TOP FUEL	W: Jim Head	R/U: Kenny Bernstein
FUNNY CAR	W: John Force	R/U: Tony Pedregon
PRO STOCK	W: Jim Yates	R/U: Ray Franks
PRO STOCK BIKE	W: John Myers	R/U: Angelle Seeling

CHIEF NATIONALS—Dallas, Texas
TOP FUEL	W: Cory McClenathan	R/U: Scott Kalitta
FUNNY CAR	W: Dale Pulde	R/U: Cruz Pedregon
PRO STOCK	W: Jim Yates	R/U: Kurt Johnson

WINSTON SELECT FINALS—Pomona, Calif.
TOP FUEL	W: Joe Amato	R/U: Scott Kalitta
FUNNY CAR	W: John Force	R/U: Tony Pedregon
PRO STOCK	W: Mike Edwards	R/U: Rickie Smith
PRO STOCK BIKE	W: John Smith	R/U: Dave Schultz

1996 Winston champs

TOP FUEL Kenny Bernstein
FUNNY CAR John Force
PRO STOCK Jim Yates
TOP ALCOHOL DRAGSTER Bobby Taylor
TOP ALCOHOL FUNNY CAR Tony Bartone
COMP Bo Nickens
SUPER STOCK Peter Biondo
STOCK Scotty Richardson
SUPER GAS John Vineyard
SUPER COMP Matt Driskell

FUNNY CAR CHAMP *John Force, the 1996 Winston Funny Car champion.*

Off-Road 1996

1996 SCORE DESERT RACING SERIES

Final Point Standings

The 1996 SCORE Desert Racing Series capped off an outstanding year by crowning several new champions, and bid farewell to one of the greatest drivers in the sport. Robbie Gordon ended his stellar off-road career by winning the 1996 Trophy Truck championship, before moving on to the fast-paced world of asphalt racing in the NASCAR Winston Cup Series. Class 10 (open wheel) buggy driver Andrew Wehe finished the season as the Class 10 and SCORE Overall Champion, with Paul Krause winning the motorcycle division.

Other big winners in 1996 included:

Mechanic of the Year: Steve Silverthorn
Engine Builder of the Year: Fat Performance
Motorcycle Manufacturer of the Year: Kawasaki
Original Chassis Manufacturer of the Year: Jimco
Journalist of the Year: Judy Smith
Photographer of the Year: Carrera
Unocal 76 Consistent Performance Awards: Jim Dizney/Don Lampus Jr
Entry Sponsor of the Year: BF Goodrich
Pit Support Team of the Year: BF Goodrich
Person of the Year: Dan Newsome

Trophy Truck

1. Robby Gordon: 354
2. Rob McCachren: 305
3. Paul Simon: 288
4. Larry Ragland: 253
5. Ed Herbst: 252
6. Curt LeDuc: 238
7. Ivan Stewart: 210
8. Jeff Lewis: 207
9. Jason Baldwin: 132
10. Javier Espinosa: 107

Results: Trucks & Buggies

Class 1
1. Brent Grizzle: 234

Class 5-1600
1. Tom Dittfeild: 171

Class 9
1. Luis Guevera: 110

Class 11
1. Victor Barajas: 115

Class 7
1. Jerry McDonald: 189

Stock Mini
1. Steve Williams: 180

Class 8
1. Dan Smith: 201

Class 1/2-1600
1. Don Lampus Jr.: 201

Class 5
1. Neal Grabowski: 171

Class 10
1. Andrew Wehe: 241

Class 3
1. Todd Gatrell: 123

Class 7s
1. Scott Stienberger: 148

Stock Full
1. Steve Olliges: 160

Pro Truck
1. Charles Harris: 275

LARRY RAGLAND *Fourth in the 1996 Trophy Truck series.*

Dirt Track 1996

WORLD OF OUTLAWS SPRINT-CAR SERIES 1996 FINAL POINTS STANDINGS

1. Mark Kinser, Oolitic, Ind	10,664
2. Dave Blaney, Cortland, Ohio	10,262
3. Sammy Swindell, Cordova, Tenn	10,058
4. Steve Kinser, Bloomington, Ind	10,017
5. Jeff Swindell, Memphis, Tenn	9,903
6. Andy Hillenburg, Broken Arrow, Okla	9,748
7. Stevie Smith, New Oxford, Pa	9,690
8. Joe Gaerte, Rochester, Ind	9,425
9. Johnny Herrera, Tempe, Ariz	9,415
10. Jac Haudenschild, Wooster, Ohio	8,512
11. Joey Saldana, Brownsburg, Ind	8,502
12. Lance Blevins, Broken Arrow, Okla	8,352
13. Jimmy Carr, Maple Ridge, B.C	7,439
14. Greg Hodnett, Memphis, Tenn	6,431
15. Brian Paulus, Mechanicsburg, Pa	5,849
16. Danny Lasoski, Dover, Mo	4,624
17. Paul McMahan, Oroville, Calif.	3,047
18. Dion Hindi, Albuquerque, N.M	2,794
19. Donny Schatz, Minot, N.D	2,556
20. Terry McCarl, Pleasant Hill, Iowa	2,363

DRIVER EARNINGS

1. Mark Kinser, Oolitic, Ind	$485,220
2. Dave Blaney, Cortland, Ohio	$310,160
3. Steve Kinser, Bloomington, Ind	$278,160
4. Sammy Swindell, Cordova, Tenn	$267,010
5. Jeff Swindell, Memphis, Tenn	$216,895
6. Andy Hillenburg, Broken Arrow, Okla	$181,215
7. Johnny Herrera, Tempe, Ariz	$175,640
8. Stevie Smith, New Oxford, Pa	$164,055
9. Joe Gaerte, Rochester, Ind	$126,895
10. Jac Haudenschild, Wooster, Ohio	$113,800
11. Joey Saldana, Brownsburg, Ind	$96,960
12. Danny Lasoski, Dover, Mo	$85,430
13. Lance Blevins, Broken Arrow, Okla	$68,030
14. Greg Hodnett, Memphis, Tenn	$60,655
15. Jimmy Carr, Maple Ridge, B.C	$51,170

CAR OWNER POINTS

1. Karl Kinser, No. 5m	10,664
2. Casey Luna, No. 10	10,262
3. Sammy Swindell, No. 1	10,058
4. Steve Kinser, No. 11	10,017
5. Two Winners, No. 7tw	9,903
6. Andy Hillenburg, No. 2	9,748
7. Dan Motter, No. 71m	9,690
8. Joe Gaerte, No. 3g	9,425
9. Gil Sonner, No. 47	9,415
10. Jack Elden, No. 22	8,422

A-FEATURE WINNERS

1. Mark Kinser	27
2. Sammy Swindell	11
3. Steve Kinser	10
4. Dave Blaney	8
5. Jeff Swindell	4
6. Stevie Smith	2
7. Johnny Herrera	1 (tie)
Andy Hillenburg	1
Billy Pauch	1
Lance Dewease	1

QUICK-TIME WINNERS

1. Mark Kinser	42
2. Steve Kinser	9
3. Sammy Swindell	5

A-FEATURE LAP LEADERS

1. Mark Kinser	810
2. Sammy Swindell	387

STEVE KINSER *Qualifying here for the Indy 500, later the same day he won a Sprint Car race.*

INDEX

MARY FRANK SCHOOL

ACKNOWLEDGMENTS

The publishers would like to thank the following sources for their kind permission to reproduce the pictures in this book:

Jere Alhadeff Photography 136, 142, 146
Allsport UK Ltd. Tim DeFrisco 115/Steve Dunn 80/Darrell Incham 25, 29/Craig Jones 47/Ken Levine 103, 112/Caryn Levy 73/Mike Powell 77b, 85, 90, 135/Pascal Rondeau 87, 93, 98/Jamie Squire 3, 52, 60, 110, 111/Matthew Stockman 92/Steve Swope 41, 54, 70, 78/David Taylor 18, 30, 34, 62, 75, 79t, 91, 101, 184
Archive Photos 15, 104
Asher Enterprises Jon Asher 16, 105-8, 113, 114, 116, 120, 123, 124, 127-129, 131-3
Centerline Photography 137-140, 144, 151, 152, 188/Paul Hanson 141, 146, 153/Robert Phillips 150
Corbis-Bettmann 11b, 67, 72, 74, 77t, 79b, 81, 99, 156/UPI 11t, 12, 66, 68, 76, 158, 160t, 161, 162b, 169,
Art Flores/IMPAC 7, 13b, 20, 22, 28, 31, 59t, b, 61, 94, 100, 101, 155, 157, 163t, 165-7, 185
Gladback Photo, Motorsports photography Jack Gladback 171, 174, 175, 177, 180, 189/Katsue Gladback 176, 179
IMS Photos 172
Indy 500 10, 71, 82, 86, 88, 96
Mark P Jacobs The Inside Track/ Speed Shots 182, 183
LAT Photographic 21
Ludvigsen 9, 19
Martinsville Speedway 48
Dozier Mobley Photography 26, 27, 32, 33, 35-40, 43-6. 49-51, 53, 56, 57
National Dragster/NHRA 109, 117, 130
Popperfoto 14
Bob Tronolone 13t, 83, 97, 159, 160b, 162t, 163b, 164, 173
Tyler Photo Illustrator Paul Tyler 178

Every effort has been made to acknowledge correctly and contact the source and copyright holder of each picture, and Carlton Books Limited apologises for any unintentional errors or omissions which will be corrected in future editions of this book.

Special thanks are due to Art Flores, for all his help, time and patience, as well as Jere Alhadeff, Jon Asher, Centerline Photography, Jack Gladback, Teresa Long (NHRA), Dozier Mobley, Bob Tronolone.